Care and Feeding
of
The Energetic Core

Karen Custer LCSW-C

authorHOUSE™

1663 LIBERTY DRIVE, SUITE 200
BLOOMINGTON, INDIANA 47403
(800) 839-8640
WWW.AUTHORHOUSE.COM

First published by AuthorHouse 08/23/05

ISBN: 1-4208-4197-1 (sc)

Library of Congress Control Number: 2005902446

Printed in the United States of America
Bloomington, Indiana

This book is printed on acid-free paper.

For the Oneness who weaves us all

The Self exists both inside and outside the physical body,
just as an image exists inside and outside the mirror.

From the *Ashtavakra Gita*

"One of the most calming and powerful actions you
can do…in a stormy world is to stand up and show your soul."

—Clarissa Pinkola Estes

Table of Contents

List of Illustrations

Acknowledgments

Books are never written in a vacuum. Without the many forms of support, encouragement and feedback from so many people, this book would have never been attempted. I have had so many wonderful teachers. (One was a very large black crow.) There is no way to list them all. The heartfelt thanks I give is in no order of magnitude.

To JR Harris of Authorhouse, I want to thank you for your friendly and helpful presense and for your speedy response to my questions and concerns. You have eased the journey.

I am deeply grateful to have known and learned from Flo Aeveia Magdalena, a true visionary in our time. Her channeling work with The Ones With No Names and The Council of Light have helped the invisible worlds become real for me. My wise meditation teacher, Shyam Bhatnagar and his perceptive disciple, Dahliana Hohé have provided me with a strong background in Hindu tradition and chakra psychology. Maxine Adelstein, a gifted healer, has given me invaluable guidance and feedback concerning energetic realities. I am also deeply grateful to Michaela Donohue who has been a much valued colleague in the field of energy healing. The opportunity to collaborate and co-facilitate with her for many years has helped to provide a crucible for me in which to distill and integrate my knowledge and experience with subtle energy.

Janice Osmann, Michaela Donohue and Cris Zocchi are three remarkable, talented and caring women who so generously agreed to be my readers. Their feedback and editing suggestions were tremendously helpful and came at a time when I could not bear to look at the manuscript one more time. Thank you is not a big enough word. Gail Borchers arrived as a last minute angel and provided me with much needed assistance with copy editing.

I also must express my deep gratitude to the adventurous people who have attended my classes on "Care and Feeding of the Energetic Core." Their questions, comments and responses were crucial in shaping this material into the form that is now in this book. Their excitement has been more of a gift than they know.

I also want to give a special thanks to Lynn Forconi, a dear friend and kindred spirit who has always been willing to delve into the spiritual world to explore, investigate and learn. Our many conversations have helped to clarify my understanding of subtle energy. She has always believed in my work and her support has meant the world to me.

And last, but certainly not least, I want to thank my husband Jerry for his unflagging emotional encouragement and help. He has indulged my avoidance of computer technology and patiently provided me with ongoing computer support.

To all of you, please know how grateful I am. You are a part of this book.

Chapter One

To Begin

The material in this book comes from a seminar series I teach, "Care and Feeding of the Energetic Core." The purpose of the course is to help people learn how to access, use, care for and protect this Core, which is the central portion of the subtle energetic system of each person. The National Center for Complementary and Alternative Medicine (NCCAM), a division of the National Institute of Health, is now calling this system the *human bio-field*. The information presented here is a synthesis from many sources. For over 30 years I have worked with numerous teachers, read, studied and pursued my own investigations of subtle energy and consciousness. During this time I maintained a private practice in psychotherapy. As my knowledge base grew, my professional work increasingly incorporated the body-heart-mind-spirit perspective. This journey has been both exciting and challenging. I found people presenting problems in therapy that required long term complex solutions from a traditional psychological standpoint but relatively simple solutions energetically. For example, some people dissociate quite easily under stress. Cognitive behavioral techniques are generally not that effective in addressing this dynamic. It is much easier to teach people to stay energetically present in their physical bodies. Some people are easily over stimulated by sounds, colors or activity in the environment. This condition can be treated with medication but it can also be addressed energetically by teaching the person how to "grow" energetic skin, which can filter out some of the stimulation.

I am not suggesting that I found a quick and easy fix for everything or for everybody. In general, energetic solutions help people who can relate to the notion of having an energetic system. What I did find during this time, however, was a clear trend: the more individuals worked consciously with these deep, subtle levels, the faster they healed and the more they opened their innate potential. I also observed that when people worked in this way, they felt empowered and better able to guide themselves.

This course is designed to provide guidelines for the development of the basic skills for self-mastery. Self-mastery, as I define it, is the ability to hold one's true center across all internal or external conditions. In other words, no matter what is happening around you—hurricanes, arguments, birthday parties—you remain balanced within yourself and retain your capacity to be present and aware. Additionally, no matter what is happening inside of you— old bad feelings, dark thoughts or great epiphanies—you remain awake and connected to your essential Self. The implications of embracing this capacity are astonishing: Once you know how to live from your Core, you can never be lost to yourself. You are always at home because home is something you have found within yourself. You are connected to your greatest clarity and to your creating Self.

Beyond the development of Self, there is an additional reason that self-mastery is important. At this point in time we appear to be in an era of great transition. Many of our traditional sources of guidance are falling apart. Educational, health, religious, social and legal systems are de-structuring. In the past, they have all served as authoritative voices, providing guidance for what was right and true. Though painful and often confusing, this de-structuring is both allowing and demanding that our reference points come from an internal source. The deep message of our time is that the ultimate guidance and authority must be found within. Who is responsible for your health, your spiritual well being, your learning, your personal relationships, your financial security? You are, of course. Self-responsibility and internal authority are sisters who travel together.

With respect to the issue of self-responsibility, I need to say that you will find no magical formulas here. As humans, we can easily become superstitious in our use of techniques as if in applying them we will be magically protected from failure and pain. Years ago as I was being wheeled into an operating room for surgery, I watched a thought skitter across my mind. "How could I wind up needing an operation? I meditate." Looking for the right way to live one's life can subtly and sometimes not so subtly be an avoidance of life itself.

Use the techniques in this book to live your life, not avoid it. A wonderful teacher once said to me, "Enlightenment doesn't mean the end of problems, it just means that you won't be rocked by them because your perspective is different." One does not need to be an enlightened being to benefit from this wisdom.

The era in which we now live is heralding a remarkable opportunity for many of us to grow up psychologically and spiritually. This maturation gives us the means to live authentic lives based, not on what we are told we are, but on who we have discovered ourselves to be. We are being asked to step forward responsibly and create our own lives and a new world, not in isolation, but in concert with the great web of life which holds every living being.

To achieve this end we must be able to be clear and recognize truth when we hear it. We must be able to release, transform or transmute that which is no longer relevant and we need to have the wisdom to know what is truly needed and what is not. We must feel secure within ourselves and be able to hear the voices of our own hearts and souls. These are all capacities that come with the development of the internal world. Going inward can be problematic for a number of reasons. First, our culture is very externalized. We have become masters of outer change. Change means new buildings, new relationships, new looks. This capacity is both our strength and our weakness. We are currently in a situation where our phenomenal technology has been developed far beyond the inner consciousness which must be used to make decisions concerning the application and use of this scientific knowledge. It is becoming increasingly clear to a number of people that the advancement of technology does not necessarily translate into progress. The context in which this technology is applied will, in fact, determine whether or not our civilization is enhanced.

One of the outcomes of the western scientific paradigm and its emphasis on the empirical method is that people have been taught to not see, feel, hear or taste the world of spirit. The inner world must be perceived by the subtle internal senses which have not generally been recognized by the scientific community. The empirical method requires the scientist to measure what he studies. Whereas this requirement is well suited to certain types of investigation, the danger here is that what cannot be quantified can be deemed unimportant. What is unimportant can become invisible.

This perspective has also influenced western religions which in turn have tended to become intellectualized and mediated by ideas and concepts. As exciting and inspiring as these ideas may be, they do not provide the experience of direct contact with the divine. The recognition has been trained away. I have met many people who say that they want to believe in Spirit but that they cannot feel it. To enter the domain of Spirit is to enter the unknown. The intellect, so finely honed in our culture, is simply not equipped to initiate this move. For that we must call upon the heart, for it is one of the best doors we have for the journey inward.

As matters currently stand, many people have a deep split within their psyches. Our spiritual traditions have recognized the human to be both animal and spirit. These aspects are not well integrated in most people. From the point of view of our spiritual evolution, I believe this integration is one of our most immediate and important tasks. Another way of saying this, is that we *are* the link between heaven and earth. Western religious perspectives have traditionally diminished the value of the animal self. Creature and Spirit are often viewed as adversaries who are at odds with one another, having vastly different agendas, or else coexisting in a disjointed compartmentalized fashion. Some people have felt forced to choose between the two. For example, in a number of both eastern and western religions, sex is viewed as antithetical to spiritual development. Physical experience is seen not as a fantastic opportunity for creative expression and growth but more as a prelude to something better once we are finished with our corporeal life. These traditions have not provided us with accurate maps or guidance enabling us to consciously access the point where spirit and matter meet— the meeting point of heaven and earth, of the non-manifest and the manifest. This is a place of dynamic creativity. We hold this connection because this bridge is part of our design. When we can recognize our subtle energetic levels, we are brought to the threshold of this vital place within ourselves.

Today there is a lot of information available on the subject of subtle energy. One can easily find books on acupuncture, meridians, auras and chakras. This material is coming from many traditions and time periods. There are translations of ancient Hindu or Buddhist texts and current spiritual practices from indigenous people around the world. There is also an explosion of publications that are channeled by nonphysical beings which cover this topic extensively.

Some of this material concerns itself with trying to establish the fact that these nonphysical states exist, while other material concentrates on creating maps or models of these levels of consciousness. The book you are now reading has been written for people who no longer need to have this level of reality proven to them but want to personally experience and work with subtle energy. By becoming actively aware and not just theoretically informed about this part of ourselves, we actually initiate a maturation and development of this subtle level. How this happens will be addressed later.

When we talk about subtle energy, we are ultimately speaking about consciousness. Consciousness, to my knowledge, has not yet been adequately defined. I consider it to be the most basic level of reality. It has aspects of energy or vibration, so it can be low, dense and limited or it can be elevated, light and expanded. Consciousness also has aspects of intelligence and awareness. Consciousness is alive. One might think in terms of consciousness as being the living force behind or within all that exists. To not be able to precisely define it, does not mean we cannot explore it. Scientists have not yet fully understood gravity and how it fits into the entire picture of the universe but when airplanes are designed, this force is taken into account. The information and exercises in this book will hopefully assist you in accelerating and increasing your level of consciousness and hopefully you will develop a "feel" for it. If you remember the sentient and alive nature of consciousness itself, you will find the exercises that are presented much more helpful and meaningful.

Deep within the subtle field is a central Core that holds both our unique essence and a breathtaking data-bank of knowledge which contains what can be termed an operations manual. For those of you who have wished life came with a set of "operating instructions," you will be happy to know that you have. They are inside of you. What you are reading is simply a "pre-manual" to help you find your own individual guidance package. To this end you will be given some very basic information on subtle energy and many exercises on how to work with your energetics. My goal has been to make this book practical and useful in an everyday sense. For example, if you want to be able to think clearly, you will have to be well grounded. If you want to be able to trust your inner hunches, your Core Alignment will have to be strong. If you keep becoming enmeshed with other people and have difficulty maintaining healthy boundaries, you will need to know how to hold your center, keep the edges of your aura firm and control the monitoring that the second chakra likes to do.

I am a person who loves detail and I hope that you will benefit from its inclusion in this work. Some of the exercises may be familiar to you but I have found that many people have difficulty getting these practices to be really effective. The foundational skills are relatively easy to learn but as with all skills, they take practice. As mentioned before, there are no magical formulas.

You must create you own life. The key is to become present, for when you are sufficiently present, you will find the necessary information for the current moment. We have been so conditioned to look for and implement the right way to master life that we have neglected a most important point: To show up and step into the flow of life that surrounds us continually. If we live from the ego, we are taken into oppression and anarchy. When we live from our Core, we walk the road to self-mastery.

Once again, the purpose of this book is to help people become more conscious of their energetic fields in practical, safe ways so that they may live more vital, authentic lives. As we become more conscious of this part of ourselves, we can begin to utilize these levels more effectively. The implications for greater levels of physical, psychological and spiritual health are truly exciting.

Go at your own pace. Take what is helpful and leave the rest. Many blessings on your journey!

Chapter Two

Introduction to Paradigms and the Model of Holism

Paradigms: Windows of Perception

Being frames of reference, paradigms ultimately determine how we look at reality and what we see. Given their far reaching effect, understanding them provides an excellent starting point from which to explore the world of subtle energetics and will help organize the specifics of our subject matter more effectively.

What is a Paradigm?

In 1962 Thomas Kuhn, a Harvard trained physicist, published an essay, "The Structure of Scientific Revolutions", and introduced the idea of paradigms. Kuhn understood paradigms to be frames of reference larger than world views, cultural perspectives or systems of thought. They included notions of reality, time, causality and the nature of creation and humankind. To grasp a paradigmatic understanding, we must know the pervasive working assumptions that are operating. Assumptions tend to be less conscious and therefore create blind spots, both literally and figuratively. Machaelle Wright relates in her book, <u>Co-Creative Science,</u> that when Columbus first arrived in America, the indigenous people were unable to see the ships sitting in the water off shore. When the sailors landed, the locals thought they had just materialized. After some weeks had passed, a few individuals began to see these structures. The first to perceive the ships were the shamans. After a while everyone could see them. The people had no internal concept of large water craft and so were initially unable to perceive them.

It is important to note that stated assumptions are not necessarily working assumptions. Most of us carry a variety of disparate beliefs at both conscious and unconscious levels. So we may intellectually hold one belief and then operate out of another. For the purposes of understanding paradigms and their influence, we must begin to look at the beliefs and assumptions that most control perceptions and behaviors, because this information will give clues about the window being used. Grasping this level in any substantial way is difficult because what we see, value and judge to be true and real is determined by the paradigmatic window through which we look. We find ourselves in the position of the proverbial fish who is looking for this thing he has heard about called water.

Shifting Paradigms

We appear to now be in the midst of a paradigmatic shift that has been slowly occurring over the past one hundred years. When there is more than one prevailing paradigm, the presence of these larger perceptual windows is easier to detect simply because of the conflicts and differences they engender. Large numbers of people will vehemently disagree with each other because different realities are being perceived. The enormous implications of this shift at both individual and societal levels cannot be overstated. What we see and what we don't determine what we do and how we go about doing it. For example, if we are using a frame of reference that assumes everything is connected in some way to everything else, we will tend to look at the interrelationship of one part to another under a number of both linear and nonlinear conditions. On the other hand, if the frame of reference assumes that people, events or objects are not inherently related but only come together under a certain set of conditions such as cause and effect, we will then tend to look for relationships *only* within that particular circumstance. Clustering of people, events or objects that are not related in this way will be overlooked or considered random coincidence. Using the first frame of reference, if I have a dream about a friend I have not seen or thought about for twenty years and she calls me the next day, I will see these as associated events. Using the second frame of reference, these same events will be deemed a coincidence and not really related to each other.

As we saw in the story of Columbus' ship, the ability to even perceive much less understand is influenced by the paradigm within which we are operating. This dynamic has implications for our study of subtle energy. Mainstream culture does not support the perception of energetic fields and this fact can strongly influence us. Many years ago when my son Ben was about three years old, he was playing in the living room when his frustrated father walked through grumbling about the family car he was trying to repair. My son exclaimed, "Daddy's red today." When I asked him what color Daddy usually was, my question startled him. "Green," he answered slowly, looking at me with a perplexed expression. "Where is he green?" I continued. Ben became self-conscious. I believe he was beginning to realize that his mother did not see what he did. He waved his hands around his head and shoulders, obviously uncomfortable. Ben refused to discuss the matter further. We have a need as humans to experience a shared reality. Many of us do not relish perceiving things that others don't. This tendency puts enormous pressure on us and I believe it takes courage to step out of the box of the consensus reality that any given paradigm will create.

These changing paradigms have been given many different names. For our purposes, I will call them the Separative and Unitive paradigms. The Separative window assumes conflict is necessary and that the fittest or best survive. The world is viewed as hierarchical and mechanistic in nature. The past influences the future in a linear, causal fashion. Within this perspective, "big" often equals powerful and the ordinary individual human is relatively insignificant and powerless. This frame of reference assumes scarcity and adversity. The large animals eat the smaller animals in a myriad of ways in an ongoing struggle to secure, protect and endure. We have used this filter to understand nature, humans and God for hundreds of years.

As we examine these differences, the dramatic impact of these paradigms come home. Issues of how we treat the environment, what constitutes good health care, how we respond to national security issues or how we define fair and reasonable business practices all become different creatures in the light of these contrasting perceptual windows. Indeed, as we will soon see, even how we define a human being is fundamentally dissimilar.

To better understand the effects of the Separative paradigm, let's look at a range of beliefs that have arisen from this window which has dominated mainstream culture:

Germs cause illness: Germs are enemies. They are invading organisms that prey on the physical body and cause disease. The solution is to kill them with antibiotics, disinfectant sprays and soaps. Farmers routinely give their animals antibiotics before any evidence of illness in order to control these germs. A casual stroll down the aisles of the grocery store reveals all sorts of products aimed at killing germs. There are personal products for the mouth, feet, female genitalia and skin that promise to rid us of these dangerous organisms. In the cleaning section, one can find air sprays, toilet disinfectant and deodorizing tablets, floor cleaners, disposable wipes that all promise to keep deadly germs under control.

Healing takes time: Healing when it occurs proceeds over time. To cure the body we have to fix things. When we are recovering, we say we are on the mend. Illnesses have their agreed-on time frames. We all know that a cold lasts for one week. I am told that bone spurs in the feet require one year to heal. Illnesses also have various prognoses. For one disease, your chances are good. For another, your chances are poor. So we know how long an illness will last and the chance of recovery. Cures that happen too rapidly are viewed with suspicion. In traditional psychotherapy a patient who recovers too quickly is said to have taken a *flight into health,* meaning that the real issues are being avoided. If a therapy technique produces effective, rapid relief, it can easily be dismissed as quackery.

Life is a struggle (No pain, No Gain): This belief is a tenant many people live by all their lives. To accept this belief is considered to be a mark of maturity. More than one of my school teachers has exhorted, "If you are not moving forward, you are falling behind!" Life is hard and must be met with effort because only effort pays off. Work comes before relaxation. Play is for children and perhaps the very wealthy. This belief when practiced in its extreme form actually can make a person feel anxious or suspicious if something comes easily.

Logic is superior to feeling: This belief holds that reason is the crowning achievement of humankind. Within this construct, we must be rational and not give sway to emotions, if we are to succeed. Answers that are logical are the ones to be relied upon. There are many people that do not live their lives under this rule and feel inferior because they do not. There are also a number of people who think they live very logically but actually do not. Many of us have had the experience of being asked why we have done something. Upon being asked, we make up a reasonable sounding answer when in fact we had no such motivation at all. We succumb to the pressure of being a person of reason.

It is better to be number 1: In a hierarchical system, the most important people are at the top. Therefore, if you want the greatest rewards, you aim for this slot or one that is as close to it as possible. This perspective breeds competition and values ambition. This window also leads to a devaluing of the people who are perceived to be at the bottom of the pecking order.

We are born and die alone: This belief is the ultimate expression of the Separative paradigm for it embraces and accepts the notion that the human experience is destined to be a lone endeavor. Separation and aloneness are assumed to be part of the basic human condition. From this frame of reference, no one thinks it odd to place a baby a few days old in a room by himself, away from his parents and his source of warmth. Death is not a community experience and most people are left to make this final transition on their own, amidst the whirling and clicking of high tech machinery.

Identifying the New Paradigm

The new emerging window is the Unitive paradigm which does not organize the world as a ladder but rather as an interconnected web. Humans, all humans, are seen as part of a larger whole. Unity underlies reality as a dynamic operative principle. Separation is not a possibility. Destroy the rain forests in the Amazon and the world suffers. Lie to yourself and everyone is hurt by this deception. Realize your creative potential and you spark this growth in others around you. Live peace and you unfold it in the world around you. This frame of reference does not command us to compete but calls us to cooperate, not out of goodness but out of necessity and practicality.

Each point on this all inclusive web is of significance and therefore, each human is seen as having power and authority by virtue of access to this web. In this paradigm when you change yourself, you influence the whole. Real power comes through being able to partner consciously with the web which is life itself. Time sense shifts with this paradigm and becomes more immediate, more focused in the now. The Internet has been said to be an apt expression of this new window. Information, both true and false, moves through the world population with breathtaking speed.

Let's review our original list of beliefs and see what shifts in light of this new frame of reference.

Germs cause illness: The Unitive paradigm agrees that germs are everywhere. They are in fact a part of life. The question becomes, why do I sometimes get a cold when I am exposed to these germs and sometimes not? One answer is that the key is in me and my immunity. When my systems are in cooperation with one another, I am strong and not open to illness. Another answer is that colds are not always a sign of weakness or poor health. Sometimes my immune system needs a workout to keep itself strong. Germs in balance are not bad.

Healing takes time: The new window does not restrict itself to linear processes and so instantaneous healing becomes a possibility. Order is still a principle of reality, but time is fluid. Events can proceed in the right order *outside of time*. The old perspective might view this as a miracle. The new paradigm would see this as a natural occurrence. Healing is about restoring balance to the system. Because the interconnected web allows access to all parts of the greater system, any number of resources can be employed in healing: herbs, surgery, prayer, intention or medication. Everything is part of life, including death. Dying in and of itself doesn't necessarily mean a person failed to heal.

Life is a struggle: The new paradigm suggests that to live life successfully doesn't require effort as much as it requires presence. To be present means to show up 100%, aware and alive. When children play, they expend an enormous amount of energy. This expenditure is not work, but a joyous, focused and engaged response to life. This natural capacity for aliveness is already within our being. I am not suggesting that the new perspective eliminates discipline, for it does not. But discipline becomes only a means to an end and not a way of life. More and more people are insisting that their work be meaningful in some way and that it be something that they enjoy. They are willing to live more simply in order to have this richness in their lives. This is a sign of the emerging Unitive paradigm.

Logic is superior to feeling: The fact that we now have training courses for developing intuition and classes and books to help people reconnect to their feeling nature suggests that this belief is beginning to change. The imbalances that are created when reason is over-valued are becoming apparent to more people. Research being done by the Heart Math group is providing evidence that de-emphasizing the head and working more with the heart-self creates greater levels of physical and psychological health without compromising the quality of problem solving capacities. This group has shown that when the electrical impulses of the heart entrain the brain, the general stress level of the body goes down. Heart rate variability (HRV) becomes even and balanced. HRV is a measure of how much the heart rate changes on a beat-to-beat basis. People who achieve this balanced rhythm report being better able to find effective, creative solutions to life's challenges. When the brain tries to dominate and set the rhythm, stress levels increase considerably and the individual becomes more reactive physiologically and emotionally. HRV becomes much more chaotic. It would seem to suggest that humans were designed to lead from the heart and not the head. The Unitive paradigm and this research group would both see wisdom as being not as the result of a reasoning process but as an expression of the combined intelligence of a balanced system.

It is better to be number 1: The new paradigm responds to this belief with the questions: At what price and to what gain? This window allows for the notion that *we are one.* The goal is not to get to the top of the heap for the best prize that exists at some point in the future, but to access the whole of life in the present moment for the purpose of creating what the greater whole is asking to birth. This latter goal may appear to be idealistic or even to some, naive, but I can tell you that what you get for this way of living is a profound sense of peace, deep joy and the most amazing occurrences—events that the old paradigm would call miracles.

We are born and die alone: The Unitive paradigm would view this belief as a deep illusion, in much the same way that the Copernican revolution viewed the belief that the world was flat. The space between people is not empty but filled with a web of profound connection. We are embedded in a world that is organic and interwoven. We all participate in this process of interweaving and the endless unfolding cycles of creation, birth and death we call life. Changes in childbirth practices such as families being present and fathers cutting the cord, reflect in a small but significant way the advent of this new window. Death, dying and the culture around this amazing transition are also shifting. More people are going home to die, surrounded by friends and loved ones. There are even groups of people who come to sing to the dying person as he or she transitions to the next level of reality.

The Separative paradigm is a stage of human evolution whose time has passed. This window was not a mistake in perception but simply a way of experiencing reality that now needs to be released. Knowing about this shift and being able to change frames of reference is a powerful way to circumvent fear or negativity. This switch is not just about thinking differently. It's about *knowing, experiencing* and *processing* differently. During an era of paradigm shifting, people will often use a mix of the two. Noticing which one you are operating in at any given moment can be extremely helpful. If you find yourself in a contracted, isolated survival mode, you are most probably operating out of the old frame of reference. Use this awareness as a little red flag that is calling you to switch your window.

Holism

Out of the new paradigm, a holistic perspective of humans is emerging. This model acknowledges four basic interrelated and interconnected levels of a person: **physical, emotional, mental and spiritual**. Although each has its own domain and function, all four are able to communicate and influence one another. When these levels are in balance, health results. The original meaning of the words health and healing involved the notion of returning to wholeness. With the coming of the mechanistic world view, healing and health became largely a matter of fixing broken parts. The paradox of our current shift is that we are both moving onto a new way of being and perceiving and *re-membering* parts of ourselves that have always been inside of us.

Brief Overview of the Holistic Model

There are many versions in the current literature on the Holistic Model, each with its own variations. They all, however, acknowledge the aspects noted above. The **physical level** refers to the physical body. The body contains intelligence which guides physical survival. It is through the body that the three other levels can express in physical reality. The physical body is the anchor point to all creative endeavors and contains an incredible amount of coded information about both you, your entire ancestral lineage, and the planet. Your body is made of atoms that were here at the beginning of time. You carry all of that experience within you physically. This constitutes no small amount of resources.

The **emotional level** is the domain of both primitive, instinctual responses and the more developed feelings such as love, compassion and peace. The emotional aspect contains the intelligence of the heart and mediates the realm of relationship. Your emotional body contains your heart's journey. You will need your heart unlocked and free to transform yourself. There is not another part of you that has this capacity for transformation.

The **mental level** consists of the entire mind, both conscious and subconscious. All attitudes and beliefs are contained on this level, as well as the intellect. Your mind, when clear and strong, gives you clarity and vision. With clarity of being comes the ability to hear the wisdom Spirit is whispering to you. Some holistic models combine the mental and emotional levels into one category and simply refer to the Body-Mind-Spirit.

The **spiritual aspect** is the part of us that is connected to the invisible, subtle level of reality. This level contains the soul which is individualized and particular to each person and the Spirit which is universal and shared by all. Both would be considered trans-personal in nature, meaning that they exist beyond the egoic, personality-based self. This aspect reflects the intelligence of intuition and direct knowing. Spirit is the architect, carrying the divine order and truth necessary to find and realize sacred wholeness. When these four are placed on a continuum, the physical level is seen as the densest part of our system and the spiritual as the most subtle.

Balance

The issue of *balance* is central to this model. When one level or aspect is either overemphasized or avoided, problems develop. We all have most preferred and least preferred aspects. Some people so love to use their minds that they neglect their bodies or their hearts. Others so focus on their feelings they don't spend appropriate time thinking things through. Sometimes an aspect is overused because it is well known and comfortable. Sometimes an aspect is overused simply because the person is avoiding one or more of the other aspects. As a result, these parts of ourselves can be strong and vital or weak and underdeveloped. When we have strong access to a particular level, then we have access to the type of intelligence that level possesses. Parts that are not adequately developed will not be able to make their contribution to the larger system. The remaining aspects are then left to compensate. While compensation can allow us to survive, it does not support the creation of a thriving life. The circumscribed equilateral cross is an excellent symbol for the perfect state of balance within our four-part system. One way to understand this symbol is that the Divine is the circle which holds the physical self, the emotional self, the mental self and the soul self. All of this is you.

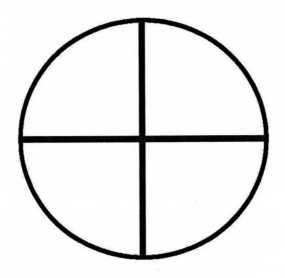

Illustration-1: Circumscribed Equilateral Cross

Exercise # 1: Evaluating your Balance

Using a circle, make a pie chart, reflecting the current balance of these four aspects within yourself. As you work through this manual, come back from time to time and reassess yourself.

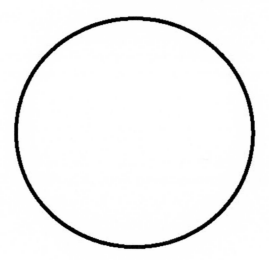

Interrelationship

In addition to balance, the dynamics of *interrelationship* are crucial to understanding holism. Go deeply enough into psychological work and the realm of Spirit will be encountered. Work with the physical body enough and feelings will surface. Every level affects every other level. How we are feeling physically affects how well we think or cope emotionally. Conversely, chronic emotional wounds are reflected both in the body and in distorted thinking. If we are afraid of Spirit or angry with God, our physical bodies, our emotional hearts and our minds will mirror these states in some way. How well we are functioning spiritually is reflected throughout the three other levels. Some holistic models suggest that the more subtle the level, the more profound its influence will be on the entire system.

These levels enhance each other when they are working in cooperation. Cooperation is achieved through the processes of *integration* and *synthesis*, which are two additional principles of holism. Integration involves bringing these aspects together, so that the body, the heart, the mind and the spirit are speaking and listening to one another. Integration is the natural progression of maturing aspects relating to one another. Lack of integration can be a developmental issue in that one level needs to be more cultivated before it can fully participate in the whole of a person. Each of us is charged with developing our weaker aspects to achieve the balance and maturation necessary for the process of integration. Your weak aspect is usually fairly easy to identify. It's the one you don't like or is of less interest to you. In the beginning just paying more attention to this particular level will bring great benefit. The other common reason for lack of integration is the presence of unresolved issues with the past which can prevent aspects from both maturing and/or coming together. Recurring negative feelings and experiences are red flags for unfinished business. (Chapter Nine contains exercises for releasing and resolving the past.)

Integration is part of any deep spiritual/psychological work. These four levels each have a contribution to make in the creation of a vital, authentic life but they must be able to communicate and cooperate with one another. This is the work of integration. Integration births synthesis. *Synthesis* results when these parts seamlessly blend and become a coherent whole. Like a flock of birds that moves across the sky whirling and changing direction as one unit, our four-part system can work with precision and unified focus. When we have achieved this state, we step into an entirely new level of power and health.

We are each responsible for finding both our wounds and our paths to healing in order to claim our wholeness. Healing is an end and also a beginning. We heal in order to live our real lives. Our real lives are about our purpose and our gifts. The whats and the hows are all coded in your body-heart-mind-spirit system, waiting to be activated. The material you are reading will help with that activation and give you the basic tools you need.

Chapter Three

Quantum Physics and Holographic Principles

Both scientists and mystics search for the most basic, unifying principles of existence. Research in the field of quantum physics, which is the study of subatomic particles and the energy exchanges that occur at these levels, appears to be offering a meeting ground for these two often opposite approaches to understanding. The sophisticated technology of holography lies in the domain of quantum physics. Research in several scientific areas is beginning to suggest that not only is the human brain organized holographically, but also that physical reality itself operates through these principles. Most of us have been exposed to holograms through movies such as *Stars Wars* or have seen them on credit and ATM cards. The implications of holographic principles are so encompassing that a general understanding of these dynamics is extremely helpful in the study of subtle energy.

In the late 1950's Karl Pribram, a neurosurgeon and brain researcher, began to apply the dynamics of holography to perception and the human brain. Pribram's work eventually took him into the field of quantum physics. His explorations and his collaboration with other cutting-edge researchers led to the notion that human physiology can basically be seen as a quantum process.

If we extend this understanding into the world of subtle energy, many dichotomies between the physical world and the spiritual domain disappear.

The Nature of Matter and Energy

Research from quantum physics tells us that all matter viewed at a subatomic level is simply vibrating frequencies of energy. Your body, the house you live in and the car you drive are all ultimately oscillating frequencies of energy. Scientists represent these undulations as sine curves (a sideways S) and measure these frequencies in hertz. A hertz is the number of oscillations that occur per second (cps). Thus, from this standpoint, the difference between color and sound is one of frequency. Audible sound is in the range of 16-20,000 cps. Visible light is registered at 429 trillion-750 trillion cps. A very common experience of the effects of different frequencies can be found with the human brain. When your brain vibrates predominantly between 16-32 cps, you are alert. If it vibrates at 8-16 cps, you feel drowsy and relaxed. The first principle of importance for our work is an understanding that at our most basic level, *we are frequencies of energy.* The implication for work with core energetics is that change comes through shifting our frequencies.

Very little of our world is random. Frequencies are arranged in patterns. Patterns are everywhere and they are interrelated. Whether the field is chemistry, music or human psychology, much of what is studied and researched can be thought of as the identification and understanding of patterns. In the past, each field has concentrated on the patterns deemed specific to its area of endeavor and there has not been much overlap between research arenas. This trend is slowly changing as the notion of interrelationship becomes more prominent in people's thinking. Interrelationship is part of the new paradigm and like the ships that sat unseen off America's shores, it will become visible to everyone at some point.

Scientists are becoming more and more aware of the far reaching effects of these interrelationships. Entire fields of study such as Chaos Theory and Environmental Ecology have come into being because of this growing awareness. This understanding has also become more widespread within the general population. The fact that changes in the Amazonian rainforest effect the weather patterns of the entire planet is now fairly common knowledge. Thus, the second principle important to our study is that *patterns are everywhere and they are interrelated.*

If ultimately everything is interconnected, then several important points emerge very clearly:

* Being alone is an illusion.
* No thought, feeling or action exists independent of the whole.
* Through interconnection, when I change one thing within myself, I influence many points in the greater system.
* Each of us must ask at some point, ""Where do I end and you begin?"

For the purposes of our work, if we remember that everything is arranged in patterns, we will be open to seeing the interrelationship of the various levels within the human bio-field and how that relates to the larger environment.

Some of these patterns are so large or so small we don't notice them. But they are here and we are part of them. Analemmas are a good example of a pattern most of us have not consciously perceived. This pattern is recorded by taking a picture of the sun every ten days for one year. Notice the shape of the analemma in the picture and see how it forms the infinity sign. When we begin to see the patterns around us, we can start to see and sense that we live in an encoded universe.

Photograph of Analemma

Analemma
Temple of Zeus, Ancient Nemea, Greece January 7, 2003 - December 20, 2003

Photograph by Anthony Ayiomamitis

Holographic Principles

The Whole is Contained in the Part

Science and the study of human energy fields have only just begun to approach one another. For now we can use our understanding of holographic principles, not as any type of scientific proof but as a metaphor for exploring the dynamics of subtle energy. As noted earlier, the theoretical direction of quantum physics has been moving toward the notion that the human brain and the universe itself operate holographically. The physics of holograms is extremely complex but a look at how a classic laser hologram is made can help us begin to grasp basic holographic principles. To create a hologram of a butterfly, a pure coherent source of light (a laser beam) is split in two. The first beam called an object beam, is reflected off the butterfly and onto a photographic plate. A second beam called a reference beam is reflected off a series of mirrors and then onto the same plate. The result is not an image of a butterfly, but a set of wavy lines and concentric circles, which is the recorded result of the interacting wave patterns from both beams. These are called wave interference patterns. When a coherent light source is directed onto the plate, the butterfly will appear as a 3-D image in front of the plate.

Interestingly, if we break the plate into a number of pieces, we can take each piece, shine the light onto it and get a 3-D image of the butterfly. These images will not be as clear and distinct but they will be complete. Each part contains the whole. If our physical world is created holographically, and science seems to be increasingly headed toward that view, then we can say that as parts of the universe, *we each contain the whole.* This second principle is important in healing because we can then assume wholeness in any human bio-field. Thus the issue becomes one of *accessing* wholeness and not creating it.

Coherency and Resonance

The second holographic principle of importance involves the effects of *coherency.* The degree of coherency in matter is the degree to which it carries purity or unified frequency. Additionally, high levels of coherency produce a dominant, cascading effect. This effect can occur within the individual or between people. Studies done with paired volunteers located in separate rooms have demonstrated this influence. These pairs were monitored by EEG readings. Each volunteer was asked to feel the other's presence. What was found was that the person who had the greatest degree of coherent brain-wave patterns tended to have the greatest influence on his or her partner, bringing him/her into a more ordered state as measured by the EEG. Another way of saying all of this is that when there are higher levels of coherency within a system, this system will be more powerful than those with less coherency.

People often talk about going about something in a half-hearted or wholehearted fashion. What they are actually referring to is the level of coherency of intent. We can feel the difference. Everything has a degree of coherency--light, matter, thought, feeling or action. This second principle is extremely important in any healing endeavor: *Greater coherency creates greater influence.* The frequency of health must be stronger than the frequency of disease for healing to occur. Effective psychotherapists have known for a long time that they cannot take clients to a level of health that they themselves have not achieved. Understanding this dynamic in light of the effect of coherency begins to explain why. This principle also suggests that in order to create or manifest anything, coherency within the creating body-- be it person, community or nation-- is a necessary prerequisite state.

Coherency works closely with the dynamics of *resonance*. Resonance can be thought of as vibrational entrainment. For example, if we place two guitars on a table and pluck the C string of one, the C string of the other will begin to vibrate sympathetically. *It is through resonance that coherency has effect.* How this applies to the dynamics of healing is that the healer must hold a high degree of coherency so that the person being healed can come into resonance with that frequency. The healer is literally modeling the vibrational frequency and the one being healed can then entrain energetically to match that frequency. This third principle also applies when the healer and the client are one and the same person.

For those who are concerned about the ethics of entrainment, and it is a valid concern, my experience has been that the one who is being entrained must at some level agree to this shift in order for it to occur. In fact, a person must want to be well for any technique or healing substance to have a lasting effect. A lack of agreement can effectively block any healing. Nevertheless, because of the power of this effect we are all deeply responsible for the kind of frequencies we carry and it behooves us to maintain as high a level of coherency as possible. How we can achieve this state consciously will be explained later.

Consciousness Affects Patterns

Roger Nelson, a research psychologist, developed a large scale experiment in an effort to find evidence that would support the existence of a collective consciousness. He initiated the Global Consciousness Project (GCP). Numerous experiments had already been done using rolling dice or coin tosses to show that random patterns can be influenced by individuals but he wanted to study the world population and the effect it would have on random number generators. To study this phenomenon researchers look for patterns that reflect a greater level of ordering than would be statistically expected as measured against pure chance. So, for example, if the generator produced "0's" and "1's", random chance would say that 50% of the time the machine would produce "0's" and 50% of the time it would produce "1's". If the percentages change significantly, then the results are deemed beyond chance and termed non-random.

Since August 1998, GCP, which is based out of a small lab at Princeton University, has recorded data from Random Event Generators (REG) that have been placed around the globe. A REG is basically a very reliable random number generator. What Nelson is finding is that these non-random patterns do in fact occur in situations that have a strong emotional component and are shared world wide. Princess Diana's funeral, the September 11, 2001 attacks on the Twin Towers and the Winter Olympics in Nagano, Japan were all events that strongly correlated to *non-random* patterns as detected by the REGs. During these periods the numbers exhibited a greater degree of ordering than would be expected by chance alone. Interestingly both strong positive and strong negative events have been associated with this effect, suggesting that powerful emotions play a role in this phenomenon.

More dramatic examples of the influence of consciousness on matter can be found in Masaru Emoto's work. In the 1990's Masaru Emoto began to photograph frozen water crystals. In the beginning he looked at pure water versus contaminated water. He took samples from all over the world. The results of his work are astonishing and the effects of environmental pollutants, graphic. Healthy, clean water crystalized into structures that were symmetrical and whole. Toxic water crystals were fractured and asymmetrical.

He then went on to expose water samples to various types of music, prayer, blessing and curses. Again, his results were remarkable. Water that was exposed to curses and negative words, such as "You make me sick. I will kill you," produced distorted, ugly crystal formations. Crystals from water that had been exposed to positive words such as "Thank You," and "Love and Appreciation," were exquisitely detailed and well formed. Examining Emoto's work in light of the fact that humans are about 80% water leads us to some interesting possibilities: Music can change us. Words are real and impact not just emotionally and mentally but physically as well. Blessing our food and drink is more than just a spiritual practice.

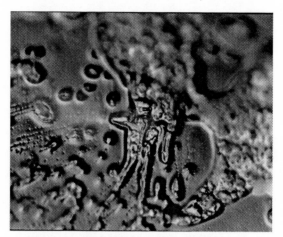

Water Crystal Photo: Effect of the words:
"You make me sick. I will kill you."

Water Crystal Photo: : Effect of the words "Thank You"

Water Crystal Photo: Effect of the words "Love and Appreciation"

Both Nelson's and Emoto's work suggest a fourth principle: *Consciousness affects patterns*. The implications of this principle for subtle energy work are enormous because it implies that the level of consciousness you hold affects every part of your being. Additionally, through the dynamics of coherency and resonance, this effect radiates into the entire environment. Each of us is literally a seed for consciousness. The strength of influence, of course, depends on the degree of coherence. The influence can be positive or negative. We can seed peace or destruction. The choice is ours to make.

Fritz-Albert Popp, a theoretical biophysicist who has studied the properties of light extensively, has postulated that coherent light and consciousness are basically the same thing. We have already determined that light is frequency or vibration. The notion here is that there is an equivalency between light, frequency and consciousness. Anything with a frequency then has consciousness. Eastern philosophy holds that everything in existence is an expression of consciousness. Within this world view, *all matter has consciousness*: rocks, planets, rivers, cells, light, animals and people. It can be said that the game of change is a game of consciousness. The key is learning how to shift it *consciously*.

Unending Relationship

Consciousness is global in nature. Before the mechanistic world view dominated our experience, people were comfortable with the notion that everything in existence was alive and aware in its own right. Indeed this way of relating to the world remains true today among indigenous populations who still honor their traditions. They speak of rock people or rock spirits, plant spirits, water and fire devas, rain gods or thunder beings. This way of perceiving reality has been termed animism and is considered by many modern minds to be primitive and naive.

I ask you to really question if this notion is in fact naive and to consider the idea that *all energy and matter have consciousness.* If you can grasp this concept, you will open perceptual gates that have been closed to most of us for a very long time. This way of perceiving is not simply about returning to old ways, as much as it is reclaiming lost abilities and integrating them into a new understanding of reality. Science with its capacity to systematically study and organize information and mysticism with its global, intuitive vision are not natural enemies. They are necessary partners whose integration creates a viable framework large enough to contain the whole of our journey.

Native American tradition speaks of a great and interconnected web. Whatever we feel, think or do reverberates across this web. To understand the enormity of this wholeness, consider for a moment the fact that scientists also tell us that the energy/matter that is here now was created at the beginning of our universe. Nothing new is here. Your physical body is made of atoms that were part of the world when the Egyptians were building the pyramids, when dinosaurs walked the earth, when Moses parted the Red Sea and when Jesus was born. How many different forms have these atoms taken? What is in their consciousness? In what ways might you be connected to these previous forms? Ultimately wholeness transcends both time and space.

Summary of Holographic Principles

* We are patterns and frequencies of energy.
* Patterns are everywhere and they are interrelated
* We each contain the whole.
* Through resonance, coherency has effect.
* Greater coherency creates greater influence.
* Consciousness affects patterns.

* All energy and matter have consciousness.

These principles provide wise reference points and guidelines from which to proceed into this most amazing level of ourselves-- our own energy fields. As we begin to work more specifically with these fields, we will come back to these principles so that you can use them in practical, concrete ways.

Chapter Four

Energy Systems

Levels of Density

To understand subtle energy systems, we need to understand that we possess what can be termed *levels of density*. Our physical world contains levels of density. Ice, for example, is more dense than water which in turn is more dense than steam. Metaphysics and Eastern philosophy have taken this principle further and maintain that all of reality is arranged in gradations from gross to subtle and subtle to gross. Within the human system we have energy structures that correspond to this continuum.

Subtle				*Gross*

Core————-Grid————Chakras——Meridians————Physical Body

The *physical* contains all the physical structures normally thought of as part of the corporal body: digestive organs, endocrine glands, muscular-skeletal structures, cardiovascular system, etc. The *meridians* which have been mapped out by Traditional Chinese Medicine are subtler pathways or channels within the physical body that circulate life force or chi within the entire system. There are some 20 basic meridians, all of which correspond to body organs. These pathways operate on a 24-hour rhythm, distributing energy. Changes within this network of energetic channels can influence all levels of functioning—physical, emotional, mental and spiritual. Interestingly, within the Ayurvedic system, very similar pathways called the Nadis, have been identified and used to enhance healing.

Chakras are found at the next level of subtlety and can best be thought of as energy centers. Many traditional indigenous systems speak to the existence of subtle, nonphysical energy vortexes within the human system. There is some variation in the number considered to be important but all acknowledge major energy centers within the head, heart and belly.

Moving more deeply into the subtle dimensions brings us to the *Grid*, which as the name suggests appears as a series of cross connecting energy lines. The Grid forms the most basic infrastructure of reality and is an interweaving of time and space. My sense is that the great web the Native Americans speak of, the Ground of Being the Buddhists refer to and the Zero Point quantum physicists talk about are all references to the Grid. Reality rests on and springs forth from this most fundamental level of creation.

Underneath the physical body, the Meridians, the Chakras and the Grid, lies the Core which is the original Self. This Self is timeless and complete. Padmasambhava in <u>The Tibetan Book of the Dead</u>, described this part of ourselves as being: "Thine own consciousness, shining, void, and inseparable from the Great Body of Radiance, hath no birth, nor death, and is the Immutable Boundless Light."

To link with this Core consciously is to return to our true selves. To possess the Core and to be in a sense possessed by it, across all transitory internal and external conditions is in fact self-mastery. When we rest within and live from our Core, we can never lose our authentic and original selves. The Core contains our guidance, our knowledge, our truth and our greatest compassion because the Core is divinity itself. When we carry the Core consciously, we become spiritual beings endeavoring to walk a human path. When we lose connection to our Core, we move into a perceived state of separation, which will always contain an element of fear. At best then, we become humans seeking a spiritual life.

The Continuum of Subtle to Gross and Gross to Subtle

Looking at these five levels as a continuum helps us see that what we are looking at is basically a comprehensive energy system of transduction and transformation. Energy from the subtle dimensions is stepped down (transduced) by increasingly dense structures—the Grid, the Chakras, the Meridians and the physical body. Energy from denser levels is stepped up (transformed) by increasingly subtle structures (the Meridians, the Chakras, the Grid, the Core). This system, which moves energy from the visible world to the invisible world and vice versa, is a linkage system between these two domains. One way to think of consciousness is that it is energy that is alive and aware. When we do that, the line between energy, light and consciousness blurs and we begin to realize that the continuum we have been discussing is really a linkage system that consciousness uses to move in and out of different states—a breathing mechanism of creation.

Five Levels of the Human Energy System

The physical body and the human bio-field that exists both within and around the physical form comprises the individual energy system. The bio-field has specific levels and functions within those levels, all of which are interrelated. Those portions outside of the physical body have been often called the aura. The easiest way to think of this arrangement is to imagine that each person is like a Russian doll which has a series of smaller and smaller dolls within it. (See Illustration-2.)

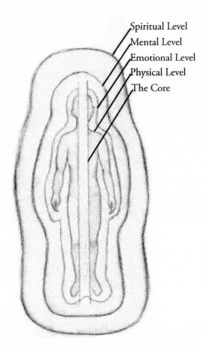

Spiritual Level
Mental Level
Emotional Level
Physical Level
The Core

Illustration-2: Five Levels of the Human Energy System

Physical Body—This portion contains everything that we would normally associate with a human body: skeletal and muscular structure, circulatory, digestive, reproductive, glandular and nervous system, etc. Note: Just outside the physical form extending approximately 1/4 to ½ inch is the etheric body or sometimes called the etheric double. This body is the most dense of the subtle bodies and the most easily seen.

Exercise # 2: Viewing the Etheric Double

To view the etheric level, place your hand on a white sheet of paper. Focus your eyes on the back of your hand and allow your peripheral vision to pick up the boundary of where the paper meets the side of the hand. Try to position the hand so that there are no shadows. Relax your eyes and try not to blink. When you first start perceiving this body, it will probably appear as a white line, outlining your hand. If you relax and wait, it will then open up to a blue band.

Emotional Body: This level can be found in the area just outside the physical body and corresponds as the name would suggest to the feeling aspect of the person. Known also as the astral body, this band is typically 3" to 6" wide, but can be as wide as 10"-12" in very emotional people. This body is intimately connected to the 2nd chakra.

Mental Bodies

Lower Mental Body: This level relates to the rational, linear mind and all functions that are associated with the intellect. Spiritual traditions call it the egoic mind. Also known as the causal body, it rests just beyond the emotional band. Again, as with the emotional body, the lower mental body can range in width, usually from 1' to 10'. The lower mental body is associated with the 3rd chakra. (Note: When the mind is mentioned in this book, the reference is being made to this lower mental body.)

Higher Mental Body: This body reflects the global, universal mind and is the part of us that is capable of gnostic or direct knowing. In esoteric systems this body is associated with the Buddhic plane. The size of this body is quite large and in some individuals can span miles. This body is connected with the upper chakras. This level does not contain the human mind but the mind of Spirit.

Energetic Core: The Core runs vertically through the center of the physical body. The Core can extend out of the top of the head and down between the legs a distance of a few feet or several miles, depending on how developed it is. The width also varies greatly, ranging from a thin line to a width greater than that of the physical body. One way to think of the Core is that it is the chalice, the vessel that contains the soul and original essence of the person.

These bodies are interconnected to varying degrees, depending on the development of the individual and the level of energetic integration that has been achieved. The goal of healing and growth is to deeply integrate the Core with the physical body, the emotional body and the mental bodies. The more integrated we are, the easier life is because we have more consistent reliable access to our inner resources. We have all had the experience of effortlessly meeting the moment with unexpected brilliance, only to meet the same circumstance later and fail miserably. What is the difference? The answer lies in access to inner resources.

The contact points where any two levels meet hold a special degree of dynamism. They are good points to target in terms of integrating and increasing coherency because change at these junctures creates the greatest level of change throughout the system. Sometimes healing must occur within a specific level before integration between levels can deepen. For example, working with emotional wounds (astral/emotional body) and beliefs (mental body) allows these two levels to integrate more easily.

Primary Contact Points

Physical Body—Core

Some of the newer alternative therapies such as Soul Recognition or Soul Retrieval are examples of modalities that heavily use this contact point. Many of the exercises in this manual also target this juncture. When these levels are integrated and coherent, we are able to embody Spirit much more fully. This integration allows us to live a soul-directed life. Systems that seek to realize an immanent spirituality focus on this connection. Immanent spirituality involves bringing Spirit into form.

Physical Body—Emotional Body

Many of the body therapies, such as Cranio-Sacral work, are now focusing on this contact point. When integration and coherency are achieved between these two levels, the person achieves emotional balance. The body is relieved of carrying the burden of the past. As a result, the physical body is freed to maintain health more easily and hold greater emotional clarity.

Emotional Body—Lower Mental Body

Psychotherapy, many meditative practices and the use of positive affirmation are modalities that make use of this juncture as an entry point to greater health. Here we find the beginning of our journey from the head to the heart. This juncture is one path to integrating the masculine and feminine aspects of ourselves. At this contact point we work with attitudes, beliefs and the corresponding feeling states they engender. We also learn the difference between being emotionally responsive and emotionally reactive.

Lower Mental Body—Higher Mental Body

This juncture has traditionally been the domain of spiritual and religious endeavors. This is where the egoic mind must surrender to the higher spiritual Self. When the individual has achieved this milestone, then there is access to the universal mind. Systems which seek transcendent spirituality place a lot of emphasis achieving coherency with this contact point. Transcendent spirituality seeks to transcend form.

Chapter Five

The Basic Chakra System

The exercises in this book work primarily with the Chakra system as an access point to the Core so basic information about Chakras is helpful to have. This information is based on a synthesis of what I have learned from a number of teachers and my own observations. We will be working with an adaptation of the yogic system from India. Even a casual study of the literature reveals there is varying opinion regarding the specific details about Chakras. For our purposes these differences should not cause undue concern.

The word Chakra means wheel. A chakra is an energy center or vortex. According to the yogic tradition, within the human body we have seven major Chakras, all of which are said to have their own minds. These minds have innate capacities and when a particular Chakra is open and activated, we have access to those skills. The abilities to love, to heal, to speak with authority and clarity, to move with grace, and to intuit are all within each of us. They do not have to be taught but merely awakened. Interestingly, probably the most basic way to open these abilities is through healthy living habits: eating pure food, getting good sleep, exercising appropriately, loving self, having meaningful work, being in caring, respectful relationships, praying and meditating. All of these practices increase and balance energy in our system and allow the Chakra system to work optimally.

As both quantum physicists and mystics have said, we live in an ocean of energy. How do we tap into these vast resources and nourish ourselves? Just as the physical body needs a variety of foods to maintain health, our bio-field needs a variety of "energy foods". Energy can come from apples and oranges or from air and light. Specific practices for individual centers will be covered later in this section. Suggestion: Pick one chakra at a time to strengthen. Try not to start too many practices at one time.

Illustration-3: Front View of Seven Basic Chakras

In addition to the seven major Chakras, we have numerous minor Chakras. They can be found in the hands and feet, in each joint and between the major Chakras themselves. As mentioned before, these energy centers serve as an interface between the subtle dimensions and the physical. They sit within the physical body and can extend beyond it.

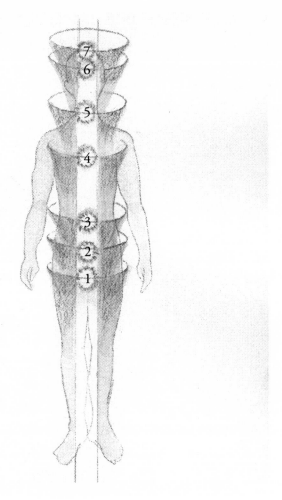

Illustration-4: Front View: Chakras Extending Beyond the Physical Body

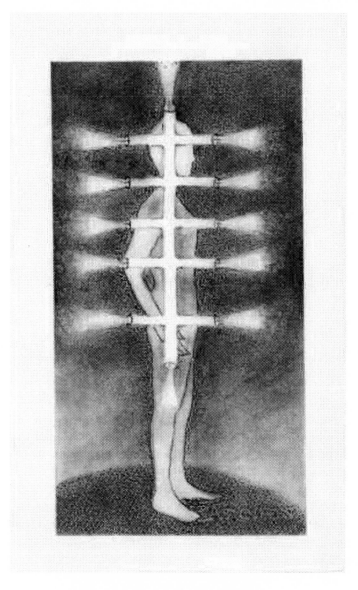

Illustration-5: Side view of Chakras

Just as meridians move energy through the human system, so do the chakras. They too work on a 24-hour cycle. Each chakra is associated with a specific endocrine gland. Within the seven centers are three channels of energy that link the seven chakras together: the left channel, the right channel and the central canal. When the energy rises, it warms the system. When is descends, it cools the system.

39

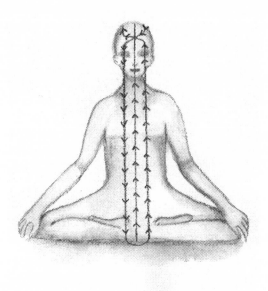

Illustration-6: The Three Channel System

Normally energy circulates by moving down the right channel and up the left. When a person is ready for the enlightenment process, energy will begin to move up the central canal. One way to understand enlightenment is that it occurs when the Core has achieved enough integration and coherency to consistently hold and reflect the higher frequencies of Spirit. Exercises that direct energy from the head toward the feet are usually safer because the system will not over heat. Meditation is a practice which encourages the energy to rise, so it is important to be properly prepared to meditate. Moving the energy upward, which is an important part of the spiritual journey, can sometimes be more problematic. People who meditate regularly will often have more problems with dry skin and hair. They will need to drink more water. (Please see Appendix 1 on Meditation.)

When the energy is moving properly, each center is nourished by the flow and is able to pass the energy to the next chakra. In this state there are balance and cooperation between the centers. If there are blockages, the flow is diminished and the chakras are not energetically fed. For example, if the third center (the seat of the egoic mind) is too greedy for energy and can't release the flow to the fourth center (the heart self), it will often store it in the neck and shoulders where the energy creates tightness and tension. The heart self is then more prone to depression and feelings of alienation because it is not being supported.

Each of the major chakras is said to possess its own mind with its own concerns, perspectives and abilities. When a particular chakra is open, energized and activated, we have access to the skills within that center. If a chakra is blocked, not adequately energized or not activated, then we will either have problems in the areas where it has domain or we will not have access to the skills the center houses.

The chakra system is designed to develop and activate over the life span of an individual. Energetic development moves slightly faster in the female and so for her, there is a sequential cycle of six years for each center. For the male, these cycles are seven years in length.

During the first seven years of a male's life and the first six years of a female's life, the first chakra is stimulated within the body. The second center is stimulated for females during ages 6-12 years and for males during ages 7-14 years and so forth. Western psychology systems recognize that little girls tend to mature faster than boys and it is interesting to note that this difference is found at an energetic level.

Energy Cycle Throughout the Life Span

	Females	Males
Chakra 1:	Birth-6 years	Birth-7 years
Chakra 2:	6-12 years	7-14 years
Chakra 3:	12-18 years	14-21 years
Chakra 4:	18-24 years	21-28 years
Chakra 5:	24-30 years	28-35 years
Chakra 6:	30-36 years	35-42 years
Chakra 7:	36-42 years	42-49 years
Chakra 1:	42-48 years	49-56 years
Chakra 2:	48-54 years	56-63 years
Chakra 3:	54-60 years	63-70 years
Chakra 4:	60-66 years	70-77 years
Chakra 5:	66-72 years	77-84 years
Chakra 6:	72-78 years	84-91 years
Chakra 7:	78-84 years	91-98 years

At age 84 for females and 98 for males, the energy stimulation starts again with the first chakra. Within the yogic system three complete rounds of energy circulations, which is considered to be the optimal stimulation for the maturation of the human bio-field, a woman would need 126 years and a man would need 144 years. This tradition views these numbers as closer to what the age span of the human body really is under ideal conditions of low stress, good diet and life style.

The chakras can be viewed as developmental steps, each with its own learning challenge. Each center has its own needs and when these needs are met in a balanced and healthy manner, then the chakra is said to be contented and it is able to release and open its innate abilities and talents.

The Seven Major Chakras

The first three chakras are personal and human in nature. They concern themselves with the human world and all that that entails. Their primary purpose and concerns are survival. The fourth chakra is a very interesting center because it has the capacity to orient itself to the manifested world or to turn itself to the realm of spirit. When activated, the fourth center or heart chakra is concerned with being of service. When the heart is turned to the world, the individual will want to be of service to others. When the heart is turned toward spirit, the desire will be to serve God. The fourth center can also function as a bridge to link the inner and outer worlds. The fifth, sixth and seventh centers are transpersonal and spiritual in nature. They do not concern themselves with the human world. Their primary function, when activated, is to connect with inner dimensions. Each center thus has own perspective and its own needs. To move through the chakra system and experience the world is like using an elevator in a high rise building. If we get out on each floor and gaze out the window, the world outside will look different at each floor.

The First Chakra

The first chakra or the root as it is sometimes termed, is located just forward of the anal sphincter and can be accessed through the base of the spine. The element it holds is *Earth*. The significance of the elements as they relate to the chakras has to do with the understanding that all of creation rests with the combining of these subtle elements. They can be thought of as basic building blocks. When a center is functioning well, then the element it holds will be able to circulate well within the energetic system. If there is disruption within a particular chakra, then there will be a problem with its associated element. The *Earth* element brings a sense of foundation or solidness.

In the ancient yogic tradition the color associated with this center is yellow. Some of the newer systems assign the color red to the root. The adrenal gland is the endocrine gland most closely related to the first chakra. This center is considered to be masculine. In general, men will be able to secure masculine centers more easily and women will be able to secure feminine centers with less effort.

This center is connected with the physical domain and all that this implies: the corporeal body, the earth and all physical matter. This chakra is concerned with physical survival—the health of our body, food, shelter and our basic life connection to those around us. When we look out into the world from the eyes of the first chakra, we are focused on those issues that relate to our physical survival: Is there food for me to eat? Do I have shelter? Can I keep myself warm? Am I safe from danger? The basic fear of the center is the fear of abandonment because from the perspective of this chakra, abandonment means death. The need of this center is for physical security. When this need has been met and contented, then this center allows us to feel safe.

When this chakra is activated and open, we feel comfortable with having a physical body. We move with grace. We are able to relax and feel at home on the earth. Our bowel function is healthy and we have a natural, uncomplicated relationship with food. We are grounded and feel secure. When our root is functioning properly, we can feel strong and substantial. This chakra is essential to the manifestation process because it is through securing the root that we bring energy into physical form. When we are rooted, we dare to place our feet upon the earth and our creative dreams into manifested reality.

Problems with this center can manifest as feelings of spaciness and basic insecurities with regard to our physical well-being. The world may feel hostile and un-welcoming which is often a projection of our own unease with the world. There can be a deep desire to not be here. This desire to not be embodied while not an actively suicidal state, is very draining to the entire system. Problems with this center can also show up as weight or food issues, poor bowel function and fears of abandonment.

Apana and the First Chakra

Apana, which means wind, is a term found in the Ayurvedic system of health from India. When it is in the first chakra, apana assists in regulating the bowels by providing the necessary wind or gas to help them move. If apana rises into the other chakras and if this situation is chronic, health problems can result. These difficulties will be in the areas where the apana is found. If it is in the second chakra, pelvic organs will be affected. Apana in the third will cause problems with the spleen, liver and stomach. Apana in the fourth can manifest as health issues with the lungs and heart. Apana in the upper centers can be very serious and cause problems with mental stability, hallucination and hearing voices.

Apana can rise for a number of reasons. Poor health and lifestyle habits and excessive fears however are the primary culprits. There are several practices that help considerably with maintaining Apana in the proper place. Cold water therapy is quite helpful. (See Appendix 2.) Regular cold sitz baths are restorative, generally invigorating and bring apana down. Years ago I met a chiropractor who was in his 90's. He was a strong, vital man and still practicing his profession. He told me that when he was 21 years old he was diagnosed with Bright's disease which is a terminal kidney condition that even today has no known cure. He was told he had less than a year to live. A friend advised him to take cold baths every day which he did. Within six months his kidneys were healed. Cold water therapy can be very powerful. In addition, regular use of The Five Rites will over time keep apana from rising. These Tibetan yoga exercises balance the entire chakra system. They take approximately 15 minutes to do. These rites also help with general levels of energy and weight problems. (See Appendix 3.)

Fear can cause apana to spike. So any practice that helps with overcoming fear can in the long term help with apana problems. For some people the fight or flight response is switched into a chronic "on" state. Medical science is just now becoming aware of the toll long term anxiety takes on the physical body. Tapping therapy can be very effective in reprogramming the brain's fear response. (See Appendix 4.) Developing witness consciousness is also vital to addressing fear patterns. (See Exercise 15.)

Tips for maintaining a healthy First Chakra

Drink plenty of fresh lemon water to keep your body well hydrated. This is especially important for meditators and energy workers who naturally conduct high levels of energy. Remember that water is a good conductor.

Establish daily morning bowel eliminations, preferably before breakfast.

Do not meditate with closed eyes if you have not had a bowel movement.

No closed eye meditation for women during their periods. (During menstruation the system is purifying itself and moving energy upward is counterproductive.)

Eat clean and healthy foods. Avoid sugar, fried foods and late night eating.

Eating with your fingers soothes your root.

Periodically use detoxification regimes or fasting, depending on the needs of your body.

Exercise regularly and get plenty of fresh air.

Walking barefoot in the early morning in grass that still has dew, stimulates the root.

Wear natural fabrics such as cotton, wool, silk or rayon. They are more supportive for your electromagnetic field.

Keep a balance of colors in your wardrobe and avoid the preponderance of any one color.

Keep your skin well lubricated with natural lotions or oils.

Avoid chemicals and preservatives both in your foods and your environment.

Regulate sleep habits. Early to sleep, early to rise.

Massage your feet before sleep.

Keep electronic equipment out of your bedroom.

Express gratitude to your body for all that it does to support you.

Practice gratitude for the opportunity to have a human experience and a human body.

Release abandonment fears. (See Exercise 19.)

Second Chakra

The second center is located between the pubic bone and the navel. The domain of this chakra is the emotional body. The associated color is orange and the element it holds is *water*. The element of water brings moisture and allows for flow in the system. This is a feminine center. The glands related to this center are the gonads. The second chakra can be thought of as the human heart, for here is the realm of personal relationship and the concerns of connection and boundaries. The second chakra also focuses on patterns of exchange. What do I want from another person? What do I do to get that? Do I ask, please, cajole, withdraw or demand? Are my transactions fair and respectful to me and others? Do I feel I have gotten enough of what I need? The health of this center will be reflected in the nature of these exchanges.

Within this center are also our sexuality, imagination and our need for self expression. When the second chakra is open and activated, these parts of ourselves will be lived in a balanced, life enhancing manner. Sex is experienced as natural and satisfying. The person is not inhibited in self expression. Showing tenderness is safe. Imagination supports creative efforts and is not used as an escape. Emotional honesty and self-responsibility, healthy sexuality and balanced creativity are the capacities held in the second center.

Problems show up in the forms of excessive daydreaming, sexual dysfunction, difficulty either giving or receiving, strong rejection issues, blocked creativity, and never feeling what one has is enough. We turn others into our parents or we try to parent them because we are unable to have an equal relationship based on love and honesty. Many people who think they have heart issues really have second chakra issues.

Clairsentience and the 2ⁿᵈ Chakra

Clairsentience is the ability to pick up on how others are feeling by feeling it yourself. A person with this capacity can sit next to someone who is sad and feel this sadness in her own body. This is an intuitive capacity of the second center and is fine as such. This can be a problem however if the person 1) doesn't know what is happening and/or 2) can't shut the perception off.

For many people who are sensitive, this is a very real issue. Going places where there are large crowds of people is exhausting. Discerning whose feelings belong to whom is unclear. If there are problems with grounding and the first chakra, the problem is compounded and the person literally becomes like a sponge for all the emotions around her.

Clairsentience can be helpful in certain situations, but it is unnecessary to get a read on every person in the general vicinity. Processing ones own emotions is enough of a task without adding everyone else's. The goal is to use this skill consciously and specifically and shut it off at all other times. If you believe you are overly clairsentient, practice the Grounding Exercises 4, 5, 6, the Light Seal Exercise 13 and Returning Energy to Where It Belongs Exercise 20, to help stabilize your system and keep your field from being too porous.

If there is an inner resistance to shutting down this mode of perception, then consider the possibility that one way you manage people is to monitor them very closely for any shifts in mood. This level of scrutiny is very draining and tends to reinforce anxiety because the behavior is basically fear driven. If you stay centered in yourself and handle what comes your way through setting appropriate boundaries, you will have much healthier relationships and you won't have to work so hard.

Tips for maintaining a healthy Second Chakra

If you have a tendency to daydream and not act, do not let yourself fantasize.

Address your co-dependency issues.

Practice emotional honesty, by being direct and clear. (Use courage here, not aggression.)

If you are inhibited, dare to self express: journal, sing, dance. You can do this in private.

Practice staying very present when someone is complimenting you or giving you a gift.

If you have trouble giving, start small and practice. Try not to expect something in return.

Be honest with yourself before automatically agreeing to do something.

Identify how you try to manage other people and then stop managing them.

Watch for any blaming attitude and stop it immediately. This is a huge power leak.

Stop personalizing other people's behavior. You are the center of your world, not theirs.

If you are clairsentient, stop monitoring people so closely.

Use the Light Seal Exercise 13 daily.

The Third Chakra

The third chakra is located in the solar plexus area between the navel and the diaphragm. Both the adrenal glands and pancreas are related to this center. The element we find here is *fire* which carries the heat necessary for life. The traditional yogic system associates this center with the color red. The newer systems connect this chakra with yellow. This masculine chakra is said to be the Sun center. Just as all the planets in our solar system revolve around our sun, when we are functioning predominantly from our third center, we will perceive the world as revolving around us. This way of perceiving is a necessary part of our development. Years ago while running a retreat, a young woman who was attending and who had problems with a diminished sense of self, came up to me. Her face was radiant with joy and she said, "I just realized I am the star of my own life." Problems only develop when we fixate on a particular center and do not move to the next one. A strong balanced third center supports self-confidence and self-acceptance. These qualities not only support us in worldly endeavors but help us with our spiritual journey.

The third chakra is the seat of the ego and the intellectual, linear mind. The road from the head to the heart, from the chakra perspective, is the journey from the third to the fourth center. The concerns of this center are ones of worldly identity and power: Who am I out in the world? How am I perceived? Do I have influence? Am I strong enough to make it out there in the world? The need of this center is for competency in order to experience self-confidence. The challenge of this chakra is to secure a healthy ego that is balanced.

In our culture, this is an especially problematic chakra. The western world in general is predominantly centered in the third but in the United States, this effect is even more exaggerated. Any cursory review of advertising and the news media shows what we value and what drives our economy: being #1, securing as much power as possible, assuming the American way is the best way for us and everyone else, striving to impress others with our possessions and lifestyle, having the most beauty, sex appeal, strength, money and intelligence. We revere the fierce competitor and the winner. In our culture the ego is constantly being over stimulated. In this overly activated state the ego becomes insatiable, striving to produce and achieve more and more in order to sustain itself. Thich Nhat Hanh, a Buddhist monk, has aptly observed that America is filled with hungry ghosts, huge beings with tiny mouths who can never get enough to feel satisfied.

The third chakra is the home of the "doer" and when this part of us dominants our system, the need to produce becomes a tyrant in our lives. Productivity, which was only intended to be a means to an end, becomes the end itself. In the Ramayana, an ancient epic from India, the Lord Ram is said to have lived a perfect human life. His listed attributes are many and among them is this one: He never engaged in more work than was necessary. The implied meaning here is that he lived a balanced life and was not caught up in unnecessary striving. He was master of his own ego.

By nature the ego has a hard time with the notion of equal partnership because it only feels safe when it has more or perceives itself as greater. The egoic mind is constantly comparing self to others: Is that person better off, more attractive, smarter, more spiritual than I am? Through comparison then the ego will always be either inferior or superior to others and will not position itself on a basis of equality. The foundation for equality is found in the upper centers. The securing and contentment of the third chakra allows us however to garner the courage to ascend within our own system to the place where we can truly meet others as equals. Problems within the third center manifest as difficulty finding our work in life, ongoing self-doubt, manipulating others by making ourselves invaluable in relationships, possessing inferiority/ superiority complexes, being power-driven, over involvement with the values of the world and competitiveness. Difficulties with insomnia, migraines, and eating issues also show up with third chakra imbalances.

When this center is operating in a healthy manner, the individual has the capacity for self-acceptance, does not need to be recognized as special, can observe the ego well and handles responsibility appropriately. In addition there is an intrinsic self respect and as a result the person does not need to diminish or inflate the self. A peace emerges and the person can truly desire happiness and good fortune for others. In classic Hindu pictures of the gods, we often see them sitting on the skin of a tiger. This image symbolizes the over coming of the egoic self. When we can sit on our own egos and not the other way around, then we have appropriate mastery of our third center.

Tips for Maintaining Health of the Third Chakra

Strengthening witness consciousness is one of the most powerful ways to help the health of this center. Use exercises in the section on awareness or refer to the reading list for books by Eckhart Tolle and Thich Nhat Hanh for practices that help with this skill.

Avoid the over use of your eyes, which stimulates this center. This includes reading, watching TV and movies.

Make time for just being. Don't let the doer dictate every minute.

Practice this exercise: Place your right hand on your solar plexus. Turn your head to the left and then very slowly rotate it to your right, trying to keep the focus of your eyes soft. Try to visually take in everything equally. When you catch your eyes focusing on something specific—let go. Notice how your eyes want to latch on.

This "grasping" is a manifestation of the ego. Be patient. You don't need to focus on achieving anything. Feel the relaxation in your body as this becomes easier and easier.

Work with strengthening your digestion. This helps the third center function properly.

Avoid drinking liquid with your meals.

Use cumin and ginger in your cooking to aid digestion.

Eat raw foods in the middle of the day rather than in the evening.

Avoid combining protein with carbohydrates. Vegetables can be combined with carbs or proteins. Eat fruit separately.

Avoid hard cheeses.

Avoid eating when angry.

Drink anise seed tea.

Use Fire breath from yoga to release anger: Inhale through the nose, expanding the belly. Then exhale hard through the mouth, contracting the belly and solar plexus. Do this rapidly until you begin to feel a "buzz". Relax and breathe normally. Then repeat several times. (Do not use this technique if you have high blood pressure or have just eaten).

Securing the first three chakras helps us to become well-balanced humans, who are capable of appropriate self-care and self-responsibility. There is an ease in the physical world. Healthy personal and professional relationships, and satisfying work become part of our experience. But we are more, much more, as we will see as we explore the world of the fourth chakra.

The Fourth Chakra

The fourth chakra is located in the chest and is considered to be feminine. One easy way to remember the chakra genders, is that through the sixth center, all even numbered centers (2, 4 & 6) are feminine and all odd numbered ones are masculine (1, 3 & 5). The thymus is the endocrine gland linked with this chakra. The element is *air* which brings movement and dryness to the energetic system. Several colors are associated with the heart: green, rose and gold. These represent, in order, the degree to which the heart is open. Within the yogic tradition it is said that there are three centers we all must secure to reach enlightenment: the first, the fourth and the seventh. These three constitute the fast track.

Here we find the realm of feeling, not the world of emotionality and instinct found in the second center, but a higher order of feeling. Within the fourth chakra is the capacity for compassion, empathy and unconditional love. The second center can be thought of as the personal, human heart, whereas the fourth center holds the universal heart. In this universal heart, we can love the children in India we have never seen. We can love an adopted child as fully as a biological child because in this heart there is no difference. If someone has not opened the heart sufficiently, he or she simply cannot love in this universal way because the connection has to be personal.

The open heart contains the healer and as a center, it has an amazing capacity to heal and transform what it touches. In the story of Don Quixote, we see a man who ventures out into the world with an open heart. Clearly this person doesn't seem to even possess a cogent mind. Don Quixote's heart sees the prostitute as a virginal maiden. But strange things begin to happen and people become what he sees. People think he is mad but he changes the world.

As noted before, this center is a bridge between the three lower human centers and three upper spiritual centers. When in pain, it can hold hatred and grief. As the heart opens, it becomes a vessel for love and compassion. With the expansion of the heart, comes a strong spiritual identity. One begins to understand that we are really spiritual beings having a human experience and not humans experiencing spirit. The ability to feel truly happy is found in this center. With this opening comes a strong capacity to nurture self and others. Intuitive abilities come forward and telling the truth becomes a necessity. At a physical level the immune system is strengthened because the thymus gland can function optimally.

Problems can come from several sources. If the heart is very open but the lower three centers are not functioning well, the individual can experience "crashes" or become overwhelmed by what the heart is feeling or perceiving.

This situation can be likened to having a huge flower on a spindly stem. There is simply not enough support there for the weight of the flower. This dynamic brings home an important point: our smoothest journey comes from having a balanced system, where all parts are performing their function.

Other problems are encountered when there are blocks or under activation. Hugh Milne in <u>The Heart of Listening</u> talks about four parts of the heart that must be claimed: 1) the Full Heart, which is our heart of high energy and the fullness of love, 2) the Open Heart, which is the willingness to be undefended and receptive, 3) the Clear Heart, which holds stillness and clarity, and 4) the Strong Heart, which is brave and courageous. If we cannot summon the fullness of heart, we simply lack the energy to activate this center. If we are not open, others including Spirit cannot touch us. If we are not clear, we will lose our way. If we are not strong, we will never take the steps we do see.

Contractions within the fourth center can cause great suffering, depression and pain because we are ultimately contracting against life. The egoic mind encourages us to withdraw from pain and the paradox is that this very shutting off creates even more suffering. Sometimes we must walk away from toxic and abusive relationships but that is not the withdrawal I am referring to. Often people stay in harmful situations because it is too terrifying to contemplate leaving them.

Alchemy and The Heart

Alchemists of old sought for the method that would turn lead into gold. The art of Alchemy concerns itself with transformation and transmutation. Transformation involves moving an element into its next evolutionary phase—a caterpillar becomes a butterfly, anger becomes passion. Higher order replaces lower order. Transmutation occurs when one element is restructured into an entirely new order—lead becomes gold, fear becomes peace. Just as the modern day electrician has a healthy respect for the energy he works with, the alchemists understood the necessary conditions for working with the powerful forces of life. They derived the alchemical principles that guided this process. One must ground, insulate and contain the necessary ingredients before heating the mixture. Only then can one hope to achieve the desired results. Within our own energetic system we have all that we need to turn the lead of our fear, sorrow and anger into the gold of peace, contentment and love.

Through our root we ground, through our second center we insulate, creating the boundaries of sacred space necessary for inner work. The intellect of the third chakra can then identify the pattern we wish to transmute or transform. The heart is the vessel into which we place the mercury of awareness. As the love and peace of the heart open, we "cook", transforming and transmuting our current states of limitation into new states of purity and creativity.

Tips for Cultivating a Healthy Heart Chakra

Practice gratitude. This is a powerful doorway to the heart. End your day with making a list of all the things for which you are grateful. You will be surprised at what touches your heart the most. Sometimes the recollection of the very simple things will have the most effect: the sunlight, the grass, the way your child giggles.

Practice prayer. Bring devotion to Spirit. Spirit doesn't need this but you do. The heart needs to love and adore fully.

Allow forgiveness. Holding on to resentments fills the heart with feelings that crowd out love. Compassion is the most natural state for this chakra and when it houses lower consciousness, there is a strain on both the physical heart and the energy center. Forgiveness is a natural stage in the healing process and one that cannot be forced. If you have someone, including yourself, that you still have not forgiven, then know that you still have work to do.

Breathe fresh air fully and deeply. The more the heart opens, the more you will need fresh air and sunlight.

Learn to talk to your heart. Greet it in the morning. As you go to sleep, ask your heart, how the day was for her. Did you listen to her today? Did you feed her? Did you give her a voice in your life. When you first start this practice, your heart may not answer. But if you continue to sit with her and draw her out with genuine inquiries about her perceptions, she will come forward.

Place your hands over your heart and breathe in light— soft golden light— send the intention to heal, restore and revitalize.

If there is any tendency to lie, clean it up. The heart does not tolerate lying and this behavior interferes with the heart's ability to open. This does not apply to what we call "white lies" such as fooling someone about a surprise birthday. Speaking truth does not require us to be cruel or offer unsolicited observations.

Laugh often and hard and at no one's expense.

Let go of the past and become present. Your true heart is found in the present.

The Fifth Chakra

With the fifth chakra we come to the first of the purely spiritual centers. This masculine center is located in the throat and is associated with element of *Akash*. In some systems this element is referred to as ether or space. This subtlest of elements brings the quality of space into creation. It is connected to the thyroid gland. The colors that are assigned to this center vary from system to system: They are blue, purple and gold.

This chakra is associated with truth, knowledge and divine order. The holographic principle that the part contains the whole is important to remember here. If you contain the whole, then you contain all eternal knowledge and truth. This center, when fully opened and activated, is the doorway to access this part of the eternal. In Hindu tradition it is said that the inner teacher resides in this center and that when we have awakened this teacher we no longer require an external one. The spiritual gifts of this center are omniscience (all knowing) and clairaudience (the ability to hear on the inner planes).

When we have fully claimed this center we have gone beyond ego and can surrender to the Divine. Our task with this chakra is to embody that surrender and live it fully in our lives. Surrender implies not resignation but acceptance of and alignment with God's will. When we truly know that Spirit does have our best interests at heart and does have a more comprehensive perspective, then living out the counsel of this deep inner voice is not about sacrifice. It's about allowing an identification with a larger Self to emerge and unfold. When we are in possession of the fifth, we can accurately reflect back to another who he or she is because we are so clear. Other abilities with this center involve the capacity to see energy fields, to be fearless, to live with gentleness and playfulness and to speak with true authority. When the mind is not in charge, we can allow spontaneous right action to flow through us.

When there is tension and tightness in the neck, this is often because of conflict in the third chakra (the egoic mind). The neck is a storage area for excess energy from the third center that is not able to flow into the fourth. If the ego is active and not surrendering the circulating energy to the heart, it will divert it to the cervical spine area and cause a "a pain the neck". Resolving head/heart arguments are very helpful in clearing this tension. Additionally, a weak first or second chakra can also throw the neck out of alignment, forcing it to compensate for a shaky foundation. The more you secure healthy functioning in your lower centers, the easier it will be for your upper chakras as they begin to activate.

Tips for Maintaining a healthy Fifth Chakra

Clear yourself of head/heart conflicts so that your fifth chakra is free to do its work of surrender.

Keep your first and second chakras strong.

Be aware of when you are "willing" things to happen. This is an inappropriate use of will and burdens this center.

Practice periods of silence. Your throat center loves silence. Unnecessary talking uses a lot of fifth chakra energy. Silence helps this center strengthen.

Chant.

Speak your truth.

Sixth Chakra

The front of the sixth chakra, which is sometimes called the Third Eye, is located in the forehead and the back of this center is in the region of the occipital lobe. There is no element associated with this center because it is said to be beyond the elements. The colors given for this center are indigo and gold. This is a feminine center and it is linked with the pineal gland. This is considered to be the chakra of self-mastery. The consciousness held within this center can take us beyond duality. When this center is activated, we feel bliss. As it opens, we are able to see beyond time and space and have the gift of clairvoyance.

As the third eye is activated, intuition opens dramatically as does the ability to move on the inner planes. Non-local (not having to be physically present) healing abilities are possible. This is the home of the spiritual teacher who teaches not so much through knowledge but by example. Lifestyle preferences are simple and the person enjoys austerities such as food fasting and silence because these practices are experienced as natural. There is no longer a restless yearning for knowledge about the cosmos because the individual experiences contentment about what is known. Great discernment is possible.

These descriptions sound amazing and they are, but there can also be fear associated with this type of sight. How many of us have difficulty simply seeing our ordinary existence with a lot of clarity much less this level of reality? Faced with the prospect of seeing God, many of us would choose to run away. When we see things as they truly are, we are confronted with the task of changing ourselves. Change is scary.

There is a reason the sixth chakra sits upon the fifth. The power of inner sight and knowing that this center contains is so great, it is really only truly safe when used for the spiritual journey. Using what we receive from the sixth center must be for serving the divine. The temptation for ego inflation is tremendous. Since the third center (the intellect) can also be very visual, the source of our information can be confusing. When we keep our sixth chakra in alignment with our heart and our Core, then we increase our chances of seeing through eyes that are both compassionate and wise. Watching for our motive in any given circumstance will help us to discern when the ego has become involved.

Some traditions discourage the development of this center because of the potential trap of egotism. My experience has been that some people have a naturally more active sixth center. If this is so, then the spiritual path will contain the sixth chakra experience of clairvoyance and its concomitant challenges.

Tips for Maintaining a Healthy Sixth Chakra

Visualization and Meditation

Practice discernment which the sixth center loves. One exercise that is helpful is to rise before first light and sit facing east to experience the beautiful and gradual coming of dawn. This stimulates the sixth chakra safely. If you chose to practice this, remember to not turn on any strong lights when preparing to sit. Night lights are fine.

The silence that you practice to aid the fifth center will support the development of the sixth. When you are quiet, you will more easily begin to discern the realm of the subtle. Read the section on awareness because awareness and discernment are sisters.

Sleep in a dark room, so that the pineal gland can rest.

The Seventh Chakra

This center is sometimes referred to as the Crown chakra and is located on the top of the head. It has no gender. Colors that are associated with this center are violet, white and the rainbow, but it is said to really be beyond color. The function of this center is to connect us to the God Self. The notion that we can directly experience God has not been a significant part of western religious belief. Fortunately, eastern tradition has preserved the knowledge of this part of the spiritual journey and it is in this center where we find the consciousness that can link us to divine levels of being.

The gifts of the crown center are contentment and omnipresence: the end of restless searching and the experience that one is everywhere. Here in the seventh chakra we find unity consciousness. All is one. From our struggle to survive, to connect with others, to find our place in the world, to serve with love, to surrender to God, we arrive only to discover we have been traveling in one great being. We were never lost. Only our narrow consciousness made our experiences seem to one of separation and conflict. Here in the seventh center we find that we are the peace and the love and the truth we have been looking for in our journey. This search is truly a cosmic game of hide and seek. In the consciousness of the seventh chakra, this is not a belief or mental knowing but a direct experience of unity itself.

The Buddhists say that we cannot really describe these higher truths in words. Words that try to explain can only convey abstract constructs and do not capture essence. Instead the Buddhists talk about "the finger pointing to the moon" and by this phrase they mean that we can only point to the existence of this level of reality. The seeker must turn inward and experience directly because it is beyond what words can convey.

Tips for Supporting the Seventh Chakra

Periodic head massage with organic, high quality oil.

Prayer, Chanting and Meditation

Practice the art of contentment in your day. Contentment is a seventh chakra state of consciousness. Cultivate it when you take a sip of water, greet a friend, slip into bed or step into your morning shower.

Be aware that the fears we hold concerning authority figures are often unconsciously projected onto the face of God. By dealing with these issues, we pave the way for embracing the Divine joyfully.

All of the tips for the previous chakras support the seventh center because when you take care of your body-heart-mind-spirit system as a whole, you take care of your crown. Enlightenment is a natural process that can be likened to pregnancy. Spiritually you have already been conceived by the Divine. In this you have no choice. Your choice rests with how you will meet this process: with resistance or with embrace. From the ego's perspective, this journey will feel as if something is being done to you. From Spirit's view, you are only meeting your Self. Know that your spiritual birth has a progression already encoded in your system, just as your genetic codes guided your physical development. By choosing to support the highest expression of the potential within your being, your life becomes an adventure into great mystery and wonderment.

Exercise # 3: Chakra Clearing and Balancing

There are a number of ways to balance and clear your chakras. The following method was taught to me by Samuel Welsh, a wonderful Earth energy worker. An Earth worker is someone who works directly with the subtle energy of the planet to help her heal and balance.

This practice is a basic maintenance process. You can use it to re-energize yourself after a stressful day or to prepare yourself for other practices. If you are an energy/body worker, you may find this exercise useful after a difficult session or if you feel you have inadvertently picked up someone else's patterns. Over time you will be able to read yourself and tell when you are out of balance and need this process.

This can be a very powerful practice and I would advise you to do this no more than once a day. For some people even this would be too much. If you find yourself getting dizzy or nauseated, try breathing more gently. The dizziness may simply be from hyperventilating. If you were not hyperventilating, the nausea and whirling sense can be a sign of very rapid release, and you may only want to do this every other day. You may want to record this exercise on a tape or use the CD that is available.

Sit or lie down with your spine straight. State your intention to clear and balance your chakras. Starting with an intention engages your whole system. You will be using your breath in this exercise. Use the breath with respect and be gentle especially with your upper chakras. Sometimes pursing your lips and running the air along the back of your throat helps direct the energy more effectively. The idea here is to clear what is ready to release. You do not want to blow out of the center with too much force.

Begin with inhaling through your nose and drawing a breath down into the root, imagining it to be a round sphere sitting just forward of the anal sphincter. Hold the breath gently in the first center and release it out the front of the first chakra, breathing out all that no longer serves you. The out breath can be through your nose or your mouth. Take another breath and again bring it to the root. Hold it a few seconds and release it out of the back of the center. Imagine you are bringing in fresh, vibrant energy and releasing anything stagnant. Now breathe in again into the first chakra and breathe out of the left side. Take another inhalation down into the root and breathe out the right side. Rest a moment and feel your root center, letting it balance and clear.

Once again draw a breath in and bring it down into the root. Try to feel the energy that rides on the breath. Now let the energy rise from the root into the second chakra which is located between the pubic bone and the navel. Hold the breathe in the second center for a few seconds and then breathe out the front of the second. Bring another breath down to the root and back to the second chakra. Hold and then breath out the back of the second center. Inhale and draw the breath down to the root. Each time you breathe in you will be bringing the breath to the first center and then letting it rise to the appropriate chakra. Let the breath and the energy rise to the second center. Hold and breathe out the left side of the second. Take another breath in, letting it descend to the first center and rise to the second. Hold and breathe out of the right side of the second. Rest and feel your second chakra, letting it balance and clear. Feel the connection between the root and the second center.

As you proceed you will notice differences between the chakras—how open they are, how much energy they take in or even how real they may feel to you. Just note these differences without judgment or comment. Stay neutral in your awareness. Let yourself just observe.

Take another breath in, breathing once again into the root, now letting the energy that rides on the breath rise up into the third chakra which is located between the navel and the bottom of the diaphragm. Hold the breath for several moments and then release it out the front of the third center, letting go of anything that is not of your true essence. You are clearing yourself of outmoded definitions of who you are. You are breathing in the present moment. Take another breath in. Take it down to the first and back up to the third. Hold and breathe out the back of the third. You are breathing off any unnecessary armor. Inhale again, going back down to the root and letting the energy rise up the third center, rising like a beautiful fountain. Hold the breath in the third and then release it out the left side. Take another breath in, breathing it down into the first chakra, letting it rise to the third. Hold for a few moments and now release out the right side. Rest for a few moments letting the third center balance. Feel the connection of the first three centers.

Let this exercise be easy. Let the breath begin to breathe you. Ride on the waves of your breathing. Now take another breath in, bringing it down to the first center and then letting it bounce up to the fourth chakra, the heart center, which is in your chest. Feel how the energy weaves the centers together as it travels from the first through the second, then the third and fourth. Each center has its own mind and this process helps these minds come together, harmonizing and balancing them. Repeat the four directions of release. Hold the breath in the fourth and breath out the front of the fourth. Take another breath, taking it down to the first, letting it come up to the fourth. Hold and release out the back. Inhale again. Breathe in light and space. Follow the energy down into the root center and back up to the heart. Hold and release out of the left side of the fourth. Take another breath in, drawing it into the root, then moving it up to the fourth center. Hold and release out of the right side of the heart center. Rest again, allowing the balancing to stabilize. Feel the heart and its connection to the other centers.

Inhale once more. Breathe the energy down into the first chakra, letting it rise to the fifth which is in the neck. Be gentle. The upper chakras are delicate. Let them open and balance. They already know how to do this. The placement of your awareness upon them activates them naturally. Hold the breath in the throat and release out the front. Take another breath in, down to the first and back up to the fifth. Hold here for a few seconds and release out the back of the neck. Take another breath. Go down to the root, bounce the energy up to the throat center, hold and then breath out the left side of the fifth center. Inhale again, breathing down to the first, going up to the fifth. Hold and release through the right side of the fifth. Rest and feel your first five centers.

Now you will clear the sixth center or third eye, the front of which is located in the middle of the brow. The back opens at the back of the head, between the ears and down to the base of the skull. Breathe down into the root. Take it up to the sixth. Hold and release gently through the brow. Take another breath in, move it to the first and then up to the sixth. Hold and breathe out through the base of the skull. Inhale again, breathing down to the root and back up to the sixth. Hold and breathe out the left side of the brow center. Take another breath in, moving it down to the first and then back up to the sixth. Hold and release out the right side of the sixth. Pause and rest a moment. Feel the connection between the first six centers.

Take another breath in, bringing it down to the root, letting it weave back up to the seventh, the crown center at the top of your head. Hold the breath and then release through the front of the seventh. Inhale again down to the root, then back up to the crown. Hold and breathe out the back of the crown. Take another breath in, going down to the first, then back up to the seventh. Hold and breathe out the left side of the crown. Repeat this for the right side. Rest and breathe. Feel the seven chakras. Let them finish balancing. Enjoy the sensation of light and breath.

Beyond the Basic Seven

We have a number of chakras in our energetic system that lie outside the physical body. These energy centers are not as well mapped out as the basic seven, but they are important to know. As more people work with them, we will come to understand them better. The information given on the upper centers is primarily from my own explorations of these centers. As you investigate your own extended system, see what you discover, for this is truly a new frontier.

The Omega Chakra

About 6" to 8" below your feet is a chakra which helps to mediate your system with the larger system of the planet. This center has been called the Earth Star or Omega chakra. Maxine Adelstein, a wonderful energy worker, first introduced me to this important energy vortex. Often people who have trouble grounding find working with the Omega chakra very helpful. (See Exercise 6.) Connecting with the Omega center helps us to feel we have something to stand on that is secure. In classic Hindu illustrations of the goddesses, they are often depicted as standing or sitting on an open lotus. Our Omega chakra can be that lotus for us, supporting us and bringing the healing frequency of the Earth into our bodies.

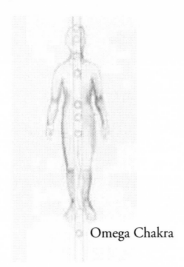

Omega Chakra

Illustration-7: Omega Chakra

Chakras Eight through Twelve

Eighth Chakra

Located 6" to 8" above the top of the head, is the eighth chakra. The eighth is the home of your Higher Self. Interestingly when someone is holding a strong connection between the seventh and eighth center, the auric field in this area assumes the shape of the pope's hat. The high arched hat is a very old design and perhaps was intended, consciously or not, to reflect this energetic connection to divine authority.

This center contains the code for your spiritual journey. The perspective from this center is purely spiritual in nature. How specific circumstances are viewed here are very different from the human view point. The loss of a marriage, a child, a career or physical health may be seen from the vantage of the eighth chakra as an important and significant opportunity. When you need to see your life from Spirit's point of view, link to your eighth center and ask to see from this perspective. The more you practice this connection and the more you are willing to really hear and see what is being communicated, the more you will be able to partner with your Higher Self in the creation of your life.

In addition, the eighth center contains the history of your spiritual patterns and past lives. People who channel and give readings on these patterns and past lives access this point. Some people are uncomfortable with the notion of reincarnation and past lives. Others have been helped considerably by exploring this possibility. The Buddha himself equivocated when asked whether or not reincarnation was true and simply said to go with what was most helpful for you.

Meher Baba, a man acknowledged by both Hindus and Sufis as a perfect master, said that from the perspective of Spirit, there is only one birth and one death. The original spark of the divine moves out from God (birth), goes through its many rounds of experiences (evolution) and then returns to God (death). From the perspective of the human, each round of experience contains a birth and death. Indeed within the lifetime of one individual there are many beginnings (births) and many endings (deaths). The most important time of your existence is now in the present moment because it is only in the present moment that you have any power to act or change. Use the notion of reincarnation only if it is of help.

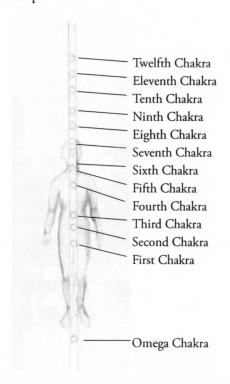

Twelfth Chakra
Eleventh Chakra
Tenth Chakra
Ninth Chakra
Eighth Chakra
Seventh Chakra
Sixth Chakra
Fifth Chakra
Fourth Chakra
Third Chakra
Second Chakra
First Chakra

Omega Chakra

Illustration-8: Extended Vertical Axis of the Core and the Chakras

The Ninth Chakra

Going up to the area 18" to 24" above the head, we find the ninth center. This is the center that houses the devas, the angelic realm and the archetypes. Within this domain we meet the idea of nonhuman intelligent forces. An archetype can be thought of as a living pattern of consciousness. Carl Jung, a Swiss psychiatrist who coined the term, was the first westerner to really explore the notion of archetypes. He believed the archetype acted as a type of window or dynamic portal that frames consciousness, allowing a particular constellation or pattern to express. Notice how there is a similarity between archetypes and paradigms in terms of how they shape what is being experienced. They both function as frames or windows that influence what subjectively registers on the psyche.

An archetype is larger than the particular person who may be expressing it. When a human expresses a specific archetype, he or she will really only express part of that pattern. The Great Mother, the Divine Child, the King, the Queen, the Healer, the Trickster, the Harlot, and the Artist would be examples of archetypes. These constellations transcend culture. They are universal in nature. One culture or time period may value an archetype more than another but the basic pattern is the same. At one time witches were portrayed as beautiful, mercurial and powerful women who could turn reality upside down and make up their own rules as they went along. We don't value witches today and they show up as old, ugly shrews, still mercurial, powerful and living life on their own terms.

Each of us will carry links to specific archetypes. They may express themselves in our lives in either positive or shadow ways. When balanced, each one holds a gift or capacity. When out of balance, each has its limitation. From a human perspective, we don't choose our archetypes. They choose us and they represent paths of consciousness we are called on to explore. From Spirit's perspective, they are yet another level of an ever expanding sense of who we are.

Another function of this center is found in its capacity to hold a group matrix. A group matrix is the structure which holds a group together. Psychologically the structure of a group involves its purpose, its accepted activities, its identity and history as well as the requirements for membership. A group matrix also has an energetic level of reality. There are times when a group becomes capable of moving as one unit, much like a flock of birds that fluidly change direction mid flight. If a strong positive matrix between the members of a group exists on an energetic level, amazing things can happen. There can be a transmission of strengths and abilities, and a seamless blending of movement and effort. Carl Jung perceptively observed that all archetypes have both positive and negative expressions. This light and shadow capacity holds true for group matrices as well.

Tenth Chakra

Moving up from the ninth about 4' to 6', we find the tenth center. You can recognize it when you get there because of its very distinctive energy which can best be likened to a magnificent golden sun that shines like sunlight on water. The feeling of this center is one of consummate compassion and peace. This beautiful solar chakra has become much more accessible over the past three years and seems to be moving closer into our energetic systems. This recent change reflects the fact that consciousness itself is growing and changing and not just the beings who are experiencing it.

Flo Aeveia Magdalena, a teacher and visionary, has said that this center contains the frequency that allows us to live and manifest from our potential as opposed to our past conditioning. So what she is saying is that one of the characteristics of this frequency is that it can act as a switch point enabling us to chose how we reference ourselves. We can live and create from our past patterns or we can live and unfold the innate potential we carry. To activate this capacity, we must open this frequency in the physical body. When we do this, we are essentially using our energetic system to unify these frequencies. This unification increases the coherency of the bio-field, which in turn enables us to embody progressively higher states of consciousness.

In the tenth chakra we come to the place where we are encoded with the first aspect of the Trinity. This center is linked with the Christos, the son of God in form. This chakra houses the blueprint for the living spirit of I AM, meaning I AM spirit in form, God in man/woman, the human Christ. I am using Christian terminology here but this is beyond Christianity. The Christos is a state of unity consciousness which Jesus embodied. For the Hindus, Lord Ram is God in form. For the Muslims, Mohammed is the perfect one. We are all encoded with the pattern of the perfected human who expresses not a repetition of past patterns, but lives the potential creativity of

Spirit. Jesus said "What I have done, so will you and more." He was able to say that because we all carry the Trinity within our system.

Eleventh Chakra

As you reach up from the tenth chakra, the next center you will encounter is deeply lunar and has again very distinctive energy. What you will find here is crystalline and cool. Assigning a spatial point of reference is irrelevant at this level because we are accessing inner dimensions. The eleventh center is the place of divine patterning, order and truth. This is where symbols exist as living structures and not representatives of mental constructs: The sacred AUM (OM) is alive and creates the world. ALLAH heals and opens mercy.

Illustration-9: AUM (OM), *Sanskrit*

Illustration-10: ALLAH, *Arabic*

As part of the Trinity, the eleventh chakra can be understood to hold the Holy Spirit or Holy Presence which is the living spiritual breath that is in all of existence. This is the center of I AM THAT. Here our identity as a human is dropped and we directly experience the I AM as being everywhere. This is the Christos of God, not humans but God. Another way of saying this is that in tenth center consciousness we know unity within our individual selves. In eleventh center consciousness, we are able to connect through ourselves to that level which rests in all of existence.

Twelfth Chakra

As we move up from the eleventh chakra, the next center we reach is twelfth which is the heart of the Mother/Father God. This third aspect of the Trinity is God the Father/God the Mother. When we touch this place, we touch the Holy of Holies. This is the center of I AM THAT I AM. Here we become GOD. There is no human, Christ, form, non-form, only one God forever unfolding in the dance. Here the individual self which we perceived in eleventh center consciousness dissolves and we become the entirety.

At a certain point in our spiritual evolution, we begin to use our fourth center as our root. We ground in our hearts. This state only comes when we have mastered our first three centers and we have learned to carry a sufficient amount of energy in our system to lift us up into the heart center in an entirely new way. When we do that and our heart becomes our root, we "ascend". See illustration 11.) This I believe is the Ascension that we are all destined for at some point in our journey. When this happens our new root is the fourth center, our seventh becomes the heart and the Christos (tenth center) becomes the crown. We have become the new human in form. Here, we have fulfilled our purpose and our destiny, because we have brought heaven and earth together.

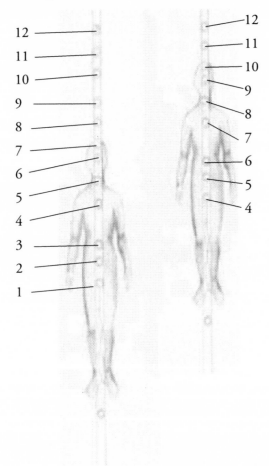

Illustration-11: Energetic Ascension

Chapter Six

The Energetic Core

The Energetic Core runs vertically through the center of the physical body and as we have noted before, comprises the most subtle portion of the human bio-field. The Core is our essence and what is left when we remove form, feeling and thought. Our Core contains our most essential light. It is through the Core and to a certain extent the grid that we are literally linked to all that is. One can think of the grid as existing as a type of super infrastructure of reality but it is the Core that holds the substance of that reality. At this level of being the distinction between me and not-me becomes much less meaningful because everything and everyone are connected. There is no separation. What is experienced is Self meeting Self. Paradoxically, one can arrive at this place in consciousness through two opposite paths: the path of inclusion and the path of detachment. Stripping away our attachments allows us to know we are not the thought, the feeling, the sensation we are experiencing. Peeling away the layers of perception and identification, brings us to a state of great emptiness. Buddhists have called this emptiness, no-thingness. Having arrived, we can know "I am nothing". Conversely we can proceed on a path of greater and greater inclusion, accepting and acknowledging everything in our experience. We accept the thought, the feeling, the sensation, the situation, the environment, the planet, the sun, the heavens. We hold all and come to know "I am everything". The consciousness of "I am nothing" and "I am everything" meet at a place where they are both true because in the deeper reality, there are no opposites.

Your access point to this deeper reality is within your Energetic Core. By working with the Core, you can activate and accelerate its development. What you gain personally is the opportunity to take the short road to wholeness and self realization. The exercises that are provided in this section are not substitutes for dealing with issues of attitude, commitment or integrity. They do however provide you with a technology that allows you to implement your choices, your truth and your commitment more effectively because you are working at such a deep fundamental level of being. Many people, for example, struggle with the issue of being fully present. Learning how to ground powerfully greatly enhances your ability to consciously be present. Practicing grounding exercises does not cause you to *choose* to be present. You must make that choice for yourself. The exercises will enable you to more effectively express and act on your choices.

Anatomy of the Core

The Vertical Axis

Within the Core are two axes. One is vertical and the other horizontal. The embodied portion of the vertical axis (VA) sits in the center of the physical body running from the crown of the head through the pelvic bowl. Depending on the individual, this axis can extend varying distances in both directions. The horizontal axis (HA) extends out perpendicularly from the vertical axis. As with the VA, the HA can range in size. As we will see, both axes have functions on personal and transpersonal levels.

The Personal Level of the Vertical Axis

We will look at the VA first because it is this axis that we must first secure. You can only work the horizontal axis effectively after you have some degree of mastery with the VA. To hold the VA, means that the areas in the pelvis and crown are energetically open and there is good energy flow between these two points. This connection constitutes what I call our alignment.

The strength of our vertical alignment largely determines the amount of clarity we hold. When our alignment is strong, our inner perceptions are less distorted and much more reliable. This axis contains the "inner operations manual" and the deep essence, so that movement toward this axis is literally movement toward our truest nature. What is meant by "inner operations manual" in this context is that just as a seed contains all the codes for the plant it will become, so the VA is encoded with all the information and knowledge needed for an individual's unfoldment and ultimately enlightenment.

This axis becomes a stable reference point that allows us to explore, deepen, heal, release and integrate energetically in the safest way possible. Living from the Core gives us a way of securing ourselves across all internal and external conditions. Achieving this state opens the door of self-mastery. What is so beautiful about this axis is that when we have found it, we can know that no matter what happens, we will never loose ourselves. We are linked to our essence, to what is most enduring. Psalms #23 reads, "Yea, though I walk through the valley of the shadow of death, I fear no evil, for thou art with me, thy rod and thy staff, they comfort me." The rod and staff represent this divine axis within you. Having found it, you may rely on it with the certainty that comes not from faith but from *gnosis* or knowing.

The vertical axis is solar in nature and has appeared in mythology as the sword or staff. On a personal level the function of this axis is to secure and hold a clear center of being. Without a center, we have no way of maintaining an integrated wholeness of self. We all need reference points on our journey and until our internal structures are consciously secured, these points will largely be external. Some people need laws and rules to guide them. So we have laws that tell us not to kill others, hit people or throw litter on the road. We have social norms that help people know what a man is and what a woman is. We have needed this structure. Without a clear center to use as a reference, however, we can overly rely on others for truth and direction. Even if we choose to go our own way, we are faced with the challenge of our own personality. Each person has many facets to the personality. These facets have a variety of levels of maturity and many of them are vying for control. With a weak internal reference point, a person is often misled by the cacophony of inner voices. Without a strong center, there is no way to sort out these dynamics and we are forced to use formulas to guide our lives. While formulas are helpful in the beginning, they eventually become traps, because at some point we will meet a situation where using our tried and true method will not work.

Securing your alignment allows you to secure your own internal guidance system which exists beyond the level of your personality. The Core is of Spirit. What we must always remember in working with our Core is that we are meeting a living consciousness with whom we co-create. The nature of Core consciousness is to evolve. Evolving to new levels of consciousness, however, requires energy. Using the practices in the Chakra Section will help your system pull in and hold more life force. In addition, practicing the alignment process given in this section will help you bring more energy into your VA. As you hold more energy in your system, you help it move to its next level of unfoldment. Strengthening the V.A. evolves in stages: 1) Opening both ends of the axis, 2) Establishing a strong energy flow between these two points, 3) Charging the axis (increasing the flow and vibrational frequency). Although the term stages suggests a notion of time, this process can happen very quickly if we are ready. The order of development does not change, but the time factor can.

Strengthening the alignment begins to activate the Core. This activation initiates several effects: 1) a widening of the axis, 2) a lengthening of the axis, 3) a raising of Core vibratory rate, 4) a unification of the Core and thus an increase in coherency and 5) developing and activating the peripheral circuitry in the horizontal axis. The VA can become wider than the physical body, though for most people this is not initially the case. At first the axis may be a very thin line of energy. As the vertical axis widens, it can begin to lengthen. The Core can move deep into the Earth and extend far above the head. Securing the embodied portion first, stabilizes the extension. What people typically encounter during this part of their practice are issues related to both their connection to the physical body and the earth and/or their connection to God and the invisible world. Raising frequency and unifying the field/Core are both actually quite easy to achieve using simple intention. Issues of control and surrender however can significantly slow down this part of the process. Working with the VA becomes both a practice used to strengthen our Core and a feedback system that tells us where we need to look at ourselves and our issues.

Imbalances in the VA show up in several typical ways and with them come concomitant difficulties. If the upper portion of the axis is significantly wider than the lower portion, the individual will be pulling in more energy and information than her system can process. This dynamic will register as confusion or over stimulation. This is the case with people who tend to be very sensitive and spaced out. These individuals will usually not like to be in places that are noisy and have large crowds. These environments are exhausting for someone who has poor grounding and a wide upper axis. This pattern is also consistent with high levels of creativity but low levels of manifestation.

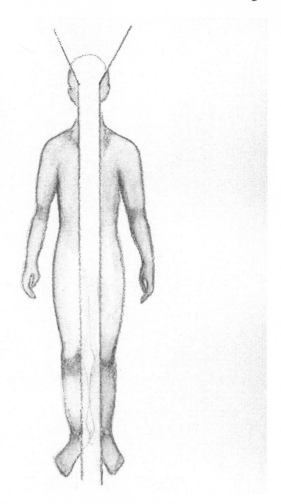

Illustration-12: Wide Upper Axis

When people are much wider or longer in the lower portion of the axis than they are at the top, then we see a pattern of difficulty in grasping the bigger picture. These individuals tend to be very focused on mundane or practical concerns. The spiritual domain will not be real to them. If spirituality is part of the life, it will not go beyond an intellectual construct. These people will not have a sense of inner guidance beyond instinct. Their focus will be on details, the concrete and the practical.

75

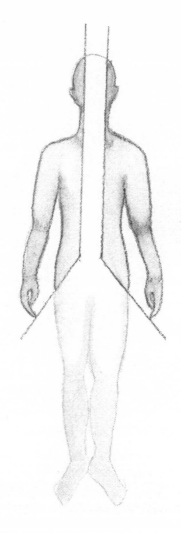

Illustration-13: Wide Lower Axis

Sometimes the two ends are shortened or constricted but the heart area is very large. When a person has this pattern, she will have a strong feeling function and tend to be big-hearted. This pattern is typical of ungrounded empaths. They absorb the pain of others but have no way to deal with the pain which they often fail to realize is not their own. People with this pattern swing up and down emotionally. They can become elated and filled with loving feeling and then crash and burn. This is the situation of the huge flower with a spindly stem. The weight of the flower head can't be supported properly and it falls over in a strong wind.

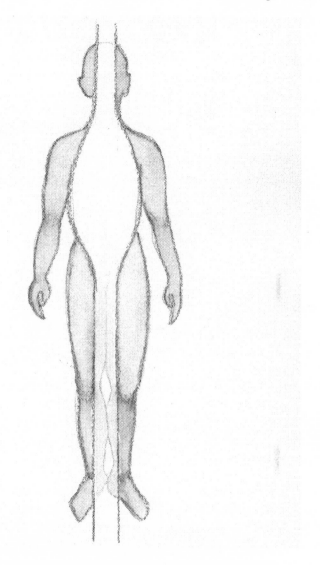

Illustration-14: Over Expansion of Heart Portion of the Core

All of these patterns demonstrate an important point. The VA needs to be opened evenly throughout the axis or it will not function optimally. The goal is to be inspired and practical, to be a visionary and productive, to feel fully and stay clear and strong. To restate, consciously working with your VA accelerates your growth and gives you greater access to your wholeness and potential. To realize and live out one's potential allows for the discovery of a deeper sense of one's being and the manifestation of one's innate creativity. We are deeply creative beings. This is our fundamental nature. People are not taught how to be creative. They are taught how to not be creative. By instilling in children limited notions of creativity, by viewing creative endeavors as frivolous and by not understanding or respecting the creative process, many of us learned to push aside this vital dimension of our nature. To stifle this force within us, in fact, can make us sick, lethargic and depressed. By developing the VA, we gain greater aliveness and joy. When we live out who we know ourselves to be, and not other people's versions of who we are, our life expands.

We have also seen that we are all connected and part of a larger whole. It is not a coincidence that in developing our Core we are participating at a much larger level in a collective journey of consciousness and evolution. In fact, it is through the claiming of this essential self that we are able to make our true contribution to the world.

The Larger Energetic System

A number of sources have spoken about the current task of the human species as being one of connecting Heaven and Earth. Remembering the holographic principle, *the part contains the whole,* we can see that the bridging of heaven and earth, or crown and root, is a reflection of a greater integration trying to occur within the larger system of consciousness. This linking translates literally into an integration of dimensions. Each energetic body and chakra represents and is connected to a dimension of reality. As we shift our systems, integrating and activating them, we affect these spheres.

Some believe this unification is our primary purpose as human beings and the greater reason for our existence. This way of understanding the dynamics of who we are and what is happening to us is appearing in many different forms and places. Brooke Medicine Eagle writes that in Native America prophecies, it has been said of the critical time we are now in, that there will be people who become pillars of light who will hold up the sky. This light will save the world. When developed, the vertical axis of the energetic Core is literally a pillar of light. Flo Aeveia Magdalena, who teaches the Soul Recognition process, says that it is through the unifying action of our Core that we both accelerate the unfoldment and creation of higher consciousness and seed it through the holographic system that holds us all. These perspectives are part of the emerging Unitive paradigm that views humans as active agents in the creation of reality.

This function is also mentioned in an interesting book entitled <u>Talking With Angels</u>. This book is a document from Hungary that was transcribed by Gitta Mallasz. It contains information four young people received from angels over a 17-month period in 1943 and 1944, when the Nazis were occupying Hungary. Several themes emerge in these writings that are significant for our study. The angels placed great importance on the issue of self-responsibility. This emphasis is quite remarkable given the powerful destructive forces that were moving through Europe at that chaotic time. If there is a clear message in our time, it is that we must become responsible for ourselves if we are to have a hope of living in a peaceful world.

The angels talked about how the world was essentially organized into seven levels. The first three worlds were called the *created* worlds of mineral, plant and animal. The last three are the *creating* worlds of the invisible force. The fourth world of the human sits in the middle. It is the abyss, the gap between the first three and the last three. This fourth world was always meant to be the *bridge* between the seen and unseen worlds. This is our destiny. The Angels called this bridging "The Act" and urged that everything must come from the Act if it is to be of any consequence. The Act implies the *realized* human or the person who has unified all seven centers within the self. This unification must be at all levels, so there is no separation between thought, feelings, sensation or action. *The bridging within the individual creates the bridging for the whole.* It is interesting to note the similarities between the seven chakras and the seven levels of the world and the urgent call to unify these spheres.

As more and more people activate their individual Cores, they become pattern makers for this new connection. Through the dynamics of resonance and coherency we are all pattern makers. Remember that we always create. The question is, what patterns do we create and open within the greater system? When we unify our Core, we become pattern makers of Unity. When we open our hearts and fill with compassion, we seed compassion in the world and yes, the universe. There is nothing here for our egos to use for inflation. This description is simply how the dynamics of our energetic system works. There is no choice about influencing and pattern making because that is an effect of our being. There is a choice, however, about what pattern or consciousness we open. As the <u>Course in Miracles</u> points out, the choice is ultimately very simple: We can choose love or fear. We can embody the light that we are or stay huddled in the littleness of our negative self-created illusions.

First we make the choice for ourselves and embody our choice in our own energy system. The choice we make for ourselves is the choice we extend to the world and everyone in it. We cannot hate ourselves and love others. We cannot live in fear and create a safe world. There is no withholding our choices from others because at this level of reality, there is no "other".

We live in amazing times, where the knowledge concerning these dynamics is pouring forth from every corner. Esoteric practices in many traditions that were once shared with only the privileged and the elite are now widely available. We now have very simple and brilliantly effective tools to help us realize Unity. Using the holographic principles of coherency and resonance, you become capable of initiating a wave of love, truth and unity that will encircle the globe. This is your basic design. In achieving this end, you are not going beyond yourself as much as you are coming into yourself.

Developing Your Vertical Alignment

Grounding

The Signature of Groundedness

When we are grounded, we can fully feel our physical body. The feet and legs are strong and stable. Our senses are operating optimally, so that colors are vibrant and sounds are clear. Grounding allows for a good sense of smell and taste. We are fully alive and our environment feels rich, immediate and real. The mind becomes quiet and clear. Time seems to slow down. Being grounded requires a well charged and open first chakra.

Many people like to be in nature because they find it restorative. Nature brings us into resonance with the Earth's frequency. People do not have to know consciously about grounding for this effect to occur. They will simply know they feel better, more relaxed and renewed. Some of this renewal comes of course from exercise, sunlight and fresh air, which are all-important sources of energy for our physical system. What is happening at a subtle level, however, is that through resonance the body is vibrationally entraining with the Earth. This entrainment is initiating a coherency within in the energetic Core.

The importance of energetic coherency cannot be over emphasized. This coherency is foundational for all inner clarity and will initiate further development of the Core circuitry. And it all begins, at least for us humans, with grounding. One of the most beautiful gifts the body can give us is this key to clarity and growth, but we cannot receive this gift if we do not join with the body fully.

The Signs of Ungroundedness

There are several types of people who have problems with being grounded. For many people who have strong spiritual interests, there is an innate preference for the world of Spirit and so for them the energy travels up more easily than down. People who do a lot of mental work can also have grounding difficulties. Again the focus here is up, not toward heaven but toward the head. The last group, and we can be members of more than one group, consists of those people who don't really want to be here. The desire to not be here may be transitory and related to a specific situation or it may be a more entrenched attitude with which we meet life. Not wanting to be here does not imply that the person is suicidal. The predominant attitude is one of life being a burden or physical existence not being worth the effort. Many people hold this attitude very subtly. If there is a distrust in life, in oneself or others, there will be an element of not participating fully in life, of not really being here. Children and adults with ADD have this dynamic. These individuals tend to hold the belief that their needs cannot be met in their environment and so it is difficult to attend. Very few people have fully opened the first energy center. Most of us can benefit by exercising the capacity to ground and be truly present. Grounded to Ungrounded runs along a continuum and is not an either/or condition.

When we are ungrounded we will function much like the joked about space cadet. The mind is distracted and cannot focus well. The body does not feel strong and solid. The feet do not seem to be fully touching the Earth. There may a clumsiness to our movements and a tendency to bump into things. There is an internal feeling of wispiness. The physical senses are not operating properly. The environment may be experienced either as dull, farther away and less solid or at the other extreme too heavy and intrusive. This latter effect is a symptom of premature ego thinning because of stress in the third center. Some people will experience this thinning when they are very tired or stressed out. Sounds or colors become irritating. There is usually however a first chakra involvement. If the root center is not stable and grounded in the Earth, it will not support any of the other centers very well. Any weaknesses in these other centers will then be exacerbated.

Grounding and the First Chakra

It has been said that since we are here in physical reality, what we bring into our energy system must be anchored into our first chakra or it will come to naught. Consciousness, ideas, energy must be linked into our root if they are to manifest into our lives. When we are anchored in our root and our energy ascends, we can link with heaven and Spirit in such a way that we become a cup for Divinity to fill. We touch Spirit, bringing it here, filling ourselves and letting the overflow radiate out for others. The connection point between our first center and our body occurs at the cellular level of consciousness. When we really know something, we know it in our body, we know it in our bones. When we want to anchor something, we can take it to a cellular level. This can be accomplished through using intention. The chapter on intention will explain in more detail how to do this.

When I work with people in session and they find a knowing inside, I ask them to feel it in their body and then make the intention that this knowing drop down to a cellular level. This step secures the work and makes it available in the future. We have all had the experience of knowing something important— that we were lovable, safe or wise— then later not being able to access this knowledge. Honor your moments of conscious awakening by linking your awareness with your body. This step is crucial. After working with this technique for a while you may begin to notice a particular sensation that comes with this practice. Make note of it because this sensation will be a marker for you, letting you know when something is integrating at a physical level. Often this integration spontaneously initiates itself. When it does not, you can help the integration take place by using intention.

The Gate of Grounding

Creation can be seen as using the circle as its basic design. We can certainly see circles or cycles in all of nature: the waves that move upon the seashore, the cycle of the seasons, the stages of our own lives. The circle also works with regard to the inner and outer realms. By grounding more deeply into the body, moving into the muscles, the bones, then the cells and the molecules, then dropping into the atoms and the subatomic structures, we can travel into the vastness of the cosmos. Here we meet the circle and a strange paradox: We can transcend the body, ascending into the highest levels of consciousness by moving through the deepest levels of the body, descending into the very same place. For those who fear being trapped in the physical body, this knowledge can be very reassuring. Grounding can bring many benefits. It is essential to both basic ordinary human functioning and advanced spiritual journeying. The physical body and grounding ultimately become a gate. Honor this function.

To Begin: Body Position

Grounding can be done from a sitting, standing or lying-down position. Practice in all three positions because you will find that it works a little differently in each. Usually we face our most challenging situations when we are in a vertical position, so it makes sense that we practice holding our grounding while we are standing or seated. Lying down is the most relaxing. This position has the advantage of being a little easier to master. You may want to record this exercise onto a tape or simply read and review the steps before doing this exercise. Most people find that working with a tape initially makes practice a lot easier. Eventually you will be able to do these exercises easily on your own. (See Resources if you would like a CD of this and other exercises.)

Exercise # 4: Basic Grounding

Begin by closing your eyes and focusing your awareness on the base of your spine. Your energy will follow your awareness. Imagine a point of light on the tip of your spine. Breathe gently as you take your awareness inside. Draw the breath into the root center, imagining that a beautiful golden light is riding on the breath. Leave the light in the first center as you exhale. You are feeding your root with energy, allowing it to take on a stronger charge.

Talk with your root center, ask it to expand, open and fill. Continue with your focus, breathing in both light and space. Wait. Use the attitude of expectancy without expectation. Notice where the root starts to respond. Perhaps it is more active in the front or the back, or maybe the left side or the right side.

There is no need for the mind to understand how all of this works. Your energetic system knows perfectly how to do this. Your task is to focus your awareness and state your request. Let your system respond. Pay more attention to the sensation of what is going on than to the visual images you are getting.

Allow the root and pelvic bowl to fill with light. Once this occurs, imagine a line or cord of energy extending from the root center into the Earth. If you are standing, the line will drop down between your legs. If you are sitting, it will drop from the base of your spine downward. If you are lying down, the line will drop down perpendicularly from your horizontal body. Ask that the line move deep into the center of the Earth, finding a clear and stable point.

Breathe energy from the Earth up the line and into your root, letting your first chakra fill. Breathe back down the line and up again, raising the Earth energy only as far as the waist. Let any overflow spill down into your legs. You are "weaving" yourself with the Earth and letting her become an extension of you. Feel the support that is there for you. An entire planet! Now ask that the vibration of the heart of the Earth open in you. Notice what happens. Allow your body to adjust. If you do not notice anything, that is okay. It does not mean that nothing is happening. You just may not be able to perceive it yet.

Give yourself time to explore this connection. Observe your reactions to it. If you detect any resistance, ask yourself to gently soften. Notice the attitudes that your mind holds. Breathe. You are breathing with the Earth. Just notice. Judge nothing. Give yourself time. This is how you open the door to feeling at home in your body. This is how you allow your body to show you its support and strength.

Once you feel you have opened and connected with the Earth, thank your body and energetic system. Thank the Earth for what she has given you. Ask your cells to memorize the sensation of grounding so that in the future you can simply remember the sensation and you will automatically strengthen your grounding capacity.

Alternate Grounding Practices

Exercise # 5: Reference Grounding

This grounding method can be very helpful for people who have difficulty connecting with the Earth. For some individuals the feeling of Earth energy causes anxiety and needless to say, this reaction interferes with any attempt to ground. When you use reference grounding, you are not actually taking in the energy of the Earth but simply bringing in the frequency. This method works on the principle of resonance, for you are allowing your system to begin to resonate in tandem with the Earth. So if the first grounding exercise was hard for you, try this one. The additional advantage of this method is that sometimes the Earth energy can be discordant, especially during these tumultuous times. If you are using the first technique and start to feel any sense of internal shakiness as you draw up the Earth energy, then switch to reference grounding.

Reference Grounding Exercise

As with the previous grounding exercise, you may sit, stand or lie down. Vary your body positions over time so that you are able to ground in all conditions. Close your eyes and take three slow and gentle belly breaths. Now imagine that you are dropping a string from the tip of your tail bone into the Earth. Aim for the center of Earth, the heart of Gaia. Remember the principle of resonance and that when two guitars are set side by side and the C string of one is plucked, the C string of the other will start to resonant. Let the string from your Root center begin to vibrate with the

85

frequency of Gaia. The vibration moves up through your string in a wave that then washes through your body. Stay relaxed. Release your body to this frequency, allowing it to reorganize and restructure your system to be in harmony with the Earth. Without judgment, feel this experience deeply. You can ask your system to "set" or click this vibration into place, so that it remains with you. Now move into your cellular level. Your mind does not know how to do this. Simply say, "Drop to cellular level," and let the rest of you facilitate that shift. Ask your cells to adjust and incorporate this frequency within their structure. Feel what happens. Enjoy the support of Gaia, mother of your physical form.

Exercise # 6: Omega Chakra Grounding

Grounding through the Omega chakra allows us to access an energetic structure that mediates our connection to the Earth. For some people, using this method feels safer and easier to do than trying to link with an entire planet. This exercise is best done standing or sitting.

Close your eyes and take three slow, gentle belly breaths. As you breathe, begin to draw your senses inward, away from the outside world. Begin to imagine that about 6" below your feet is a beautiful, open lotus flower or golden disc which is at least 1 foot in diameter. Open your first center and imagine energy flowing down your legs and into your feet. Let the energy begin to grow roots out of the soles of each foot and extend to the Omega chakra. Breathe up from the Omega and into your feet. Now breathe from your feet into the Omega center. Keep the feet very relaxed. Remember, use no effort, just let the process happen. Your system knows how to do this. Continue this breathing exchange between your body and the Omega center, including more and more of your legs until the entire lower part of your body is connected and breathing with the light below your feet. Now extend a line of energy from the Omega into the Earth. Feel one long continuous connection from your pelvic bowl to the center of the Earth. Enjoy. When you are ready, take this vibration into your cells and let them vibrate and dance with Gaia.

Additional Exercises for the Root Chakra

The Pear

The Pear is a process that can be used when the energetic pattern is wider at the top than the bottom. Generally the goal is to keep the energy centers equally open to create balance in the system. This technique is essentially an over correction but is quite effective. This overshoot is similar in principle to what is used in karate board splitting. The person aims not at the board itself but at a point slightly beyond the board thus avoiding any hesitancy.

The Pear is used not as a maintenance practice but can be used effectively as an adjustment. This method brings the energy down from the head and into the hips. We all have energetic habits or chronic ways in which we sit energetically in our bodies. In western culture with its overemphasis on speed and mental pursuits, we are constantly pulling energy into our heads. Over time this emphasis can cause imbalances. The following situations are examples of when The Pear can effectively be used:

* When negative thought patterns are triggered and the volume of the internal critic is high.
* When you are over stimulated mentally and your thoughts are racing or you are feeling uncomfortably rushed.
* You are having symptoms such as obsessive thoughts or impulses.
* If you are caught in spiral of recurring shame.

John, a man I worked with, had an energetic tendency to be top-heavy and reported periodic episodes of having disturbing impulses. He would be sitting with someone and have the urge to kick the other person in the shins. John was aware of a general agitation and restlessness but was not angry with the person. These thoughts and impulses were alarming to him. When he began using The Pear process in these situations, he found he was able to regain a sense of calmness and the upsetting impulses stopped. This type of symptomatology is quite common with Obsessive Compulsive Disorder (OCD). The Pear process does not cure this disorder but can be an effective technique to ease through OCD flare ups. People with OCD chronically have too much energy in their heads.

Another woman, Ellen, was struggling with a strong internal negative voice that regularly told her she was a loser, no one liked her, and that she would never amount to anything. We all have an internal critic, but Ellen's was so loud and toxic, she would become immobilized with despair and shame. She began using The Pear when under attack and found over time that she could control the volume of the critic's voice quite effectively. Having some distance from the critic allowed her to be more objective and less under the influence of this negativity.

Exercise # 7: The Pear

Breathe into the lower part of your body, imagining that you are expanding into a pear shape. (For women who are self conscious or concerned about feeling too big, remember this is only happening energetically.) Put all your awareness in your hips. Let your head vanish. On the in breath, expand the bottom of the pear. On the out breath, sink deeper into yourself. You are a standing, walking pear. The calmness you seek is at the bottom of this pear. Maintain this shape as long as you need to.

Exercise # 8: The Whirl

The Whirl is a method for manually opening the root chakra. Although the effect with any one practice session will be only temporary, over time this exercise encourages it to stay open and helps you to become more conscious of when it has closed.

While standing or lying down, place your right hand over your pubic bone. The edge of your thumb should be at the top of the bone. Pull your hand 1" away from your body very slowly. Lightly touch your hand back on the pubis. Do this several times until you begin to sense a connection staying in place when you move your hand off your body. Keep your hand relaxed. The air will feel warm or "thick" or perhaps your hand will tingle. These are all signs that you have made an energetic connection. Now you can begin the Whirl. Gently pull your hand away 1" again. Slowly move your hand in little clockwise circles. To make sure it is clockwise, start with the hand over the pubic area and move to the left. Drop down and circle to the right, coming back up to center. Continue for several minutes. You should feel an opening in your hips and more energy in the pelvic bowl. Vary the rate of speed with your whirls, noticing which is best for you. Repeat as often as necessary.

The Alignment Process

There are a number of traditions that address the vertical portion of our energetic system. I have found it in Hindu practices, esoteric Egyptian practices and Native American practices. This alignment process helps you secure the vertical axis within your energetic matrix and is one of the most powerful ways you can strengthen yourself energetically. Since it is such a basic foundational practice, I recommend that you use this exercise regularly.

Please note the importance of keeping the tube equally wide at the top and bottom. As noted earlier, when there is a wider opening at the top, there is a tendency to bring in more energy, light, information than the system can process. When a person is experiencing this dynamic, she will usually feel spaced out or confused, as if there is too much going on. More is not better. If the bottom is wider, the person will feel grounded but somewhat clueless. What you want is to be able to clearly process what you bring into your system. When the crown and the root are equally open that is exactly what you get!

One of the hardest parts of practice is keeping the experience fresh. Once we have done something a number of times, we tend to assume we know all about it and that there is nothing new to be learned. Nothing can be farther from the truth. Use what the Zen masters have called the beginner's mind: This session is your first. Whatever you have learned thus far is limited, so set it aside and begin again. In this way you will find great depth in your practice.

This exercise also initiates a clearing and unifying of the subtle energy fields. This effect is natural because as you return to your basic essence vibrationally, you will begin to let go of energetic patterns which no longer serve you. Your field becomes more coherent. Coherency translates into unity. This effect relates to the holographic principle discussed earlier. The sound master I studied with once said that an enlightened person's brain held cells that were all vibrating at one frequency. It has been said by a number of sages that we all have a true tone and if we could let go of all the other noise we carry around and just be with our true note, we would be home.

You will probably notice that some practice sessions are much easier than others. Difficult sessions can simply be feedback that you are stressed, tired or have "wandered" off center. If a particular practice session has not felt productive, know that it still brings benefit.

Exercise # 9: Basic Alignment

Practice suggestions: This practice can be done standing, sitting or lying down. The main idea is to have a straight spine. Lying down is usually the easiest position to start with because you can relax yourself more readily. Do practice in the other body positions as well, because as with grounding, you will find that the alignment works a little differently in the various positions. Since we usually meet our greatest challenges when we are either standing or sitting, being able to hold alignment in these positions is important. Some people find that using music is very helpful and if music makes this process more powerful for you, then use it. But also practice without it, because again many of our challenges emerge when music is not playing in the background. To prepare yourself, wear comfortable, loose clothing and drink plenty of water. With good levels of hydration, you will be able to "run" the energy through your system more easily.

Once you know how to align yourself, you can practice in many settings: while standing in line at the grocery store, while taking a walk, while waiting for a bus or while taking a shower. In addition, try to be aware of this part of yourself at least in some measure as you go about your day. In this way you will be training yourself to access this level of reality as you live your life. Most of us are very busy and do not have a lot of extra time to set aside for formal practice. With this work you really do not have to do too much of that and it is far better to integrate your practice into your day.

1. *The first step in alignment is to secure your grounding using your preferred method.*

2. *Now let your root remain open and bring your awareness to the crown of your head. Focusing lightly, ask the crown to open and expand to a width that is no wider than the opening you are holding in your root. Breathe softly through the top of your head, imagining that the top of your skull is melting into light. Give your system time to respond to your request. Adjust the root and the crown until they are equally open. If the root is smaller than the seventh center, try closing the crown chakra a bit.*

3. *After securing both the root and crown, split your focus so that you are aware of both points simultaneously. Hold this awareness. As you do, you will stimulate the connection between these two points. As this connection strengthens, a line or column will appear or be felt. This is your alignment matrix and your energetic Core. It runs down through the center of your body, not along your spine. Some people have trouble at first trying to practice simultaneous awareness. It will become easier with practice.*

4. *Once you have the line or tube (it will widen over time), begin to fall back into this line, breathing light, breathing energy into the tube. Just the way you built a charge in the root, now build a charge in the entire tube. Breathe directly through the sides of the tube. Breathe down through the opening in the crown. Breathe up from the ground through the root. As you breathe up, bring the energy from this direction first into the base chakra and then if you wish up to the heart center. When breathing energy up, take it only as far as the heart chakra.*

5. *As you bring a full charge into the tube, let it widen. Staying referenced to the tube, sit in the heart. Remember simultaneous awareness. Begin to visualize a large ball of golden white light above your head. Let the light stream down through the tube and all around the body. Focus on the light. Let yourself become light,*

*light that is pouring down filling the tube, filling the physical body
and then flowing into the Earth. Know that the tube can become
a column that is wider than your body. Let it expand naturally.
Invite it to do so. Let yourself be patient. Patience is not a matter
of endurance but trust. Trust your own energetic system to fill
itself out.*

6. *As you become liquid light, bring this light into the cells of your body.
Ask that the cells begin to vibrate at the same rate of speed as the
light. Notice the feeling and sensation of this experience. You are
beginning to unify your field as you do this, for you are bringing
a vibrational congruency into your system. Identify the sensation.
Gently hold this part of the process and let the unification open.
If you find any places that are sluggish or not connecting, simply
observe, focus in the heart and breathe in more light. It is natural
for some parts to unify more quickly than others.*

7. *Let yourself gently move, staying aware of your alignment. Open
your eyes slightly, keeping a soft focus. Walk a few steps in your
alignment. How does this feel? Now open your eyes fully and slowly
look around the room, not focusing on anything in particular. Use
soft eyes. Gaze at your surroundings from deep within your Core.
This is Spirit looking out into the world. Feel the receptivity and
clarity that is here. Stay referenced in your alignment. Let the
world open and come to you. What does the world show you in
this moment?*

8. *Take your alignment into your day or your night, noticing what it is
like to live from this place.*

Extending Your Vertical Alignment

Once you are able to align and unify chakras 1-7, you are ready to begin
working with extending your vertical alignment to include your Omega
chakra, the heart of the Earth and your upper centers 8-12. The best way to
approach this extension is to do it in a balanced fashion. So you would use
the basic alignment process and work with unifying the Omega through the
eighth chakra, then move down to the heart of the earth and then go back to
pick up chakras nine, ten, eleven and twelve. Each chakra has a distinctive feel

and energy to it. Go up the ladder individually so that you begin to recognize their unique energy signatures. Consolidate your extension as you go along by breathing energy down into your physical body from the center you are working with, so that the Core remains strong and stable.

The Horizontal Axis

This axis holds the point of interface with the outer world. Through this axis we feel our connection to others and our environment. The HA is lunar in nature and relates to the time-space continuum. If we can liken the VA to a rod or sword, then we see in the horizontal axis the chalice or bowl. Truly these two axes are our own chalice and sword, the divine forces of the feminine and masculine. When we balance this axis with our vertical axis, we create the ground for the emergence of the divine androgyne or the divine marriage. From that union comes the cosmic Self who is capable of an entirely different level of living. Along this axis we encounter duality—the place of polarities and opposites: female and male, past and present, light and dark, inner and outer. And because we meet them here, we can also resolve and integrate them here.

When we extend our field out, we do so on the horizontal axis. If our VA is very strong and clear, then this extension is healthy and energizing. If there is a good balance between the two, then we become a chalice or container that can heal and transform what it holds. If we extend out without a strong VA, we will experience fragmentation and depletion. We will also tend to take on the frequency and patterns of those around us. Another way to say this is that if we do not have a strong reference to our inner alignment, we will begin to reference and resonate with the frequencies outside of ourselves. If we are maintaining the vertical axis properly at the same time we are expanding our HA, we can remain in our truth and compassion and connect profoundly with others.

We can feel when someone has an expanded H.A. This person will seem to fill the room. We can sense the extension of energy. Performers who have a strong stage presence and relate well to the audience, have large HAs. A number of years ago while attending a concert one evening, I observed the bio-fields of the musicians. One of the performers seemed to be a column of light standing on the stage. The quality of the light was very pure and clear, reaching up far beyond his head. The next performer who played the piano had a huge field that almost reached to the back of the hall. After the concert, I listened to people discuss their reactions to the performers. The pianist was very popular and many positive comments were said about him. The first performer was described as technically proficient but cold and colorless. At the time I wondered what people would have experienced if the first performer had been able to energetically touch his audience. Stage presence is not just a psychological phenomenon, but also an energetic one. Yet, true mastery of our Core involves more than just being able to hold these two axes for a performance. We must be able to live in an ongoing way from this dynamic balance within ourselves.

Just as we need to unify the frequencies between our root and our crown and between heaven and earth, so do we need to unify the frequencies between the left and the right and the front and the back of our HA The native American practice of calling in the seven directions of the East, the South, the West, the North, the Earth, the Sky and the Heart, reveals a deep understanding of the need for balance within these two axes. This practice also reflects the wisdom and knowledge of the powers of the heart to heal and quicken the process.

Blending and unifying the left and the right is often about balancing the female and male energies within us. For most people the right side is associated with the masculine and the left side is related to the feminine. Being able to sense energy flow on these two sides can tell you a lot about how these two forces of masculine and feminine move in your system.

Blending the front and the back is often about releasing the past and filling with the present. Most people carry a much higher vibration in the front of their bio-field than in the back. This situation can arise for a number of reasons. First, we simply tend to be more aware of what is happening in front of us, so we will address and clear what is there. Second, when we "put things behind us" but don't really let them go, they follow us wherever we go—out of sight but definitely not out of influence. As a result, a lot of unfinished business waits for us, if we would just turn around. When the energetic frequencies in the back of the bio-field are denser and more primitive, we will experience a sense of not being backed up by life. We will carry a feeling of unease. By unifying these frequencies and clearing the denser energies, we bring a much greater sense of comfort to ourselves. In addition, by widening our awareness to include our back portion, we encourage the development of what mystics call "spherical vision" or 360-degree sight. The exercises on Spinning and Back Combing given in this section are very good for this portion of your Core.

When the HA is accessed through the heart, a universal womb is tapped into which can hold and transform the world. As with the VA we must first start with our own world, our own inner polarities, before we can truly bring benefit to the greater whole around us. Because this axis involves the time-space continuum, when there is mastery within the HA, this axis can be used for non-local or long distance healing. This means that the healer can facilitate the healing without being physically present. Many energy healers and shamans work in this way. There is a level within the HA where the outer and the inner world meet and this is the point of the HA that the healer accesses.

Exercises for the Horizontal Axis

Exercise # 11: Back Combing

If you have a lot of dense energy in the back portion of your field, try the back combing exercise before spinning. You will find that it helps quite a bit. Back Combing is very simple. In addition to creating better spinning work, it will help you feel more backed and supported by the universe. Any lack of coherency in the field will register at some level as discomfort. This is also a good general maintenance exercise and after you have mastered it, can be done very quickly. Check the back of your field periodically to make sure it is carrying a frequency similar to the front.

Establish your grounding and alignment. Imagine that above your head is a beautiful large sun or star of golden white light. The light begins to radiate and pour down over your back and through the space behind you. Relax and let this light wash through your field, helping to release, transmute or transform anything that is dense or that you no longer need.

Open your back and let the light "comb" you. Take your time. Let the light do the work. Your job is to be present and receive. Breathe and experience this deeply. Ask your Core and your physical body to adjust themselves to this new lightness.

Exercise # 12: Spinning

This exercise was taught to me by Flo Aeveia Magdalena and is good for safely developing the horizontal axis. Spinning is an energetic tool that helps with the circuitry that runs perpendicular to the Core. This exercise balances the left, right, front and back of your field. Many people tend to store things they don't want to look at in the back part of their field. You may experience a surge of seeing aspects of yourself that you don't normally encounter. This effect may not necessarily occur while you are practicing the exercise. Material can surface later in the day or through dreams. While this result may be unsettling, try to welcome it. You are clearing, balancing and unifying your field with this process.

Set your vertical alignment in place. Once you have practiced this, you will be able to do this very quickly. Let the Core become a very bright line of energy that extends deep into the earth and as far above your head as you comfortably can. Then imagine a stream of golden white energy coming out of your left bicep, moving in a circle in front of you to your right. It then turns and proceeds behind you, coming back to the area just in front of your upper arm. This circle is being made outside of your physical body at the level of your heart center. As you first practice this exercise, you will discover your areas of thick or dense energy. This practice will help you clear these areas. If you run into these thicker areas and have difficulty moving the stream of energy through, you can get a little creative here. Sometimes using a spinning golden ball or a flying swan helps, as does using an undulating movement within the spin. The main point is to not use effort or force to move energy through. Use whatever image works for you. Experiment and enjoy.

Keep the circle going round and round. This movement is your spin. At first you will want to keep the circle close in and by doing so you will be working primarily within your emotional body. As the circle becomes smoother and smoother, you can slowly let it move out. If you lose the spin, simply start up another one.

At some point in your practice of this exercise, you will begin to feel a pulsation. This occurs when the levels of the various subtle bodies begin to weave together and integrate. You don't need to make this happen. It will happen naturally. Then let go of the notion of spinning and let yourself pulsate with the love and the truth that you are.

Your Core as a Balanced Unified Whole

Your Core is a brilliantly designed system that allows for the descent of Spirit and the ascent of Soul. In this way the Core houses the biblical Jacob's ladder. Another way to say this is that when the vertical axis is aligned in a strong clear manner, the ladder is in place. When the horizontal axis is open and balanced with the VA, the portal for healing and creation is present. Within the human system, Spirit has a window into matter and matter has a passageway into enlightenment. This energetic matrix provides the structure or temple for spiritual immanence and the vehicle for spiritual transcendence. When these two axes are in balance and connected, we begin to function as holographic orbs of light.

When the vibratory frequency is kept high, the Core will be in a state of radiance which keeps the Core evolving. The light of this radiance is living consciousness, cosmic presence. This radiance provides tremendous protection for the Core. Low energy states tend to attract other low frequencies. In spiritual dimensions, like attracts like. Until radiance is easily maintained, other energetic practices of protections are recommended. (See Light Seal exercise at the end of this section.) As noted earlier, when the Core is ready an ascension takes place. The fourth chakra becomes the root of the energetic system. Chakras 1-3 begin to function more in the fashion of the Omega chakra. The entire energetic system shifts up the ladder. As the fourth center becomes the root, the fifth becomes the second, the sixth becomes the third, the seventh is the new fourth, the eighth becomes the fifth, the ninth becomes the sixth and the tenth becomes the new seventh. There is now a direct link with the Trinity of the Christos, the Holy Spirit and the Mother/Father God. Now the Holy Spirit functions as the higher self. The one who has undergone this ascension or enlightenment is now a cosmic being. This cosmic being is rooted in the heart. This shift occurs not only within the VA but in the HA as well. Remembering the notion of the Russian doll and its succession of smaller dolls, we can visualize that these levels are now blending so that there is no longer separation within the energetic system. As the system matures and moves toward enlightenment, the spiritual, mental and emotional levels that were discussed in Chapter Four integrate and become more tightly woven. There is strong coherency within both the VA and the HA which are now able to communicate with and support one another. The now consolidated energy system has become unified. The physical body itself vibrates with the frequency of the unity that the system has achieved.

Energetic Protection Exercise

Exercise # 13: The Light Seal

This exercise is very good for providing energetic protection. I learned this method from Christel Nani, a medical intuitive and healer who is based in California. This technique helps to seal energy leaks in the etheric body and to protect the integrity of the Core. Use it daily when you first begin to practice. Once you become accustomed to maintaining a good seal, you will be able to recognize very quickly when it has become compromised. A sudden drop in general energy level is often an indicator that the seal has weakened.

It is important to know that you are not creating a wall with this exercise as much as enhancing your energetic skin. The function of healthy skin is to keep what is supposed to stay on the outside, outside, and what's supposed to stay inside on the inside. Healthy skin is a permeable barrier and selectively filters what comes into the system. Your light seal has the same function. This exercise strengthens the etheric double which we worked with in Exercise # 2.

Begin with closing your eyes and taking three deep belly breaths, letting the exhalations be longer than the inhalations. Now imagine that you have a highlighter pen that marks with a brilliant golden white light. Start at the top of your head and begin to trace the outline of your body. Go down the right side of your head, neck and over the top of your right shoulder. Trace the pen down the outside of your arm to the end of your little pinky finger. Try to feel the energy. Ask that as you move the pen, any leaks or tears in your etheric body be immediately sealed. Continue tracing around all of your fingers and thumb on the right hand and then come up the inside of the arm. Stop and feel the line you have created so far. Begin again going down the right side of your torso, over the hip and down the outside of your right leg to the ankle bone. Move the pen along the edge of the foot to the little toe. Trace around all the toes and come up the inside of the right foot. Draw the line up the inside of the leg to the groin and cross over to the inside of the left leg. Continue to feel and imagine this bright light sealing the etheric body. Trace down to the ankle bone, up to the left big toe and then around all the other toes. Move the line along the outside of the left foot to the ankle bone and then up the outside of the left leg. Trace over the hip and torso. Stop and feel the outline that you have created so far. Continue to the armpit and go down the inside of the left arm to the thumb. Trace around the thumb and all the fingers, coming up to the outside wrist of left hand. Highlight the outside of the left arm, going up across the shoulder, up the side of the neck and the left side of the head, and ending where you began.

Now imagine that you have a large water color brush. Starting at the front, on top of your head, you sweep the brush from one side to the other, painting and blending the light over your face, down your neck and the front part of your body. Paint under your feet and up the back of your legs and the back of your body until you reach the top of your head. Feel the entire seal very vividly. Ask for the seal to complete itself. Now ask that the vibrational frequency inside of your physical body raise to match the vibration of the seal. Let that happen. Just stay present and give this part a little time. Feel the effect. If your HA tends to overextend, take a deep breath in and pull it closer to your physical body. This is especially important if you are overly empathic or clairsentient. Feel yourself consolidate and strengthen.

Chapter Seven

Awareness as a Meta-Tool

One of the key meta-tools for growth and self-mastery is *awareness.* Awareness connotes consciousness or knowing. This capacity is often associated with light. In colloquial terms we say, "The light dawned on me," "The light bulb went on in my head," or "I saw the light," each meaning that a new level of awareness has occurred. Spiritually, we speak of an enlightened person and understand that this individual knows in a way that we do not comprehend. Even in the secular use of the term enlightenment, we know that this reference is to a state of greater or more comprehensive knowing.

There is a Zen story about a student who seeks out a famous teacher to ask him what the three most important things are in finding enlightenment. The teacher agrees to answer his question and replies, "The first most important thing is Awareness. The second most important thing is Awareness. And the third most important thing is—-Awareness." Awareness is a capacity that is both exquisitely straight forward and mysteriously complex and subtle. Awareness is an art.

This capacity, often confused with thinking and analyzing, paradoxically involves not thinking at all. There is a Zen saying that "to the extent you are thinking, you are not aware." In the Zen tradition, which is very rich in its study of awareness, there is a teaching tale about an art student who went to study with a master. The teacher met the boy and proceeded immediately with the first lesson. He took the student into a courtyard and then, placing a fish in front of him, said, "I want you to look at this fish and tell me what you see. Look carefully. I will be back." The master left for several hours. The boy looked at the fish, noticing the eyes, the way the color was darker on top and lighter on the belly. He saw it had a tail, fins and scales. When the teacher returned the boy reported his inventory. The teacher bellowed, "You haven't seen this fish at all! Now I want you to really look!" And this time he left the boy for three days.

At first the boy looked and didn't see anything different. However, the teacher took so long to return that the student became completely bored. After awhile there was nothing to do but stare at a fish which was beginning to smell rank. As he gazed at the fish, he began to see there were dozens of colors in front of his eyes—not just the obvious ones of light and dark, but a vast number of shades of blue and gray and white. Amazed, he found patterns in the scales and he noticed the proportions of the fish's body and their relation to one another. After three days he found many details that had eluded him in his first session with the fish. When the teacher finally returned, the student excitedly told him all the things he had noticed about the fish. "Yes," said the teacher nodding his head slightly. "You have begun to see the fish."

Awareness is like a light we can shine onto anything. The more aware we become the deeper we can penetrate reality and the more we can embrace the totality of the moment. *One of the most amazing characteristics about awareness is that it has the capacity to change what it touches.* Physicists have seen this phenomenon in their experiments with subatomic particles and know the observer affects what is being observed. Healers who work with subtle energies are quite familiar with this phenomenon. Awareness at its purist level is alive and vital.

Attending as the First Prerequisite to Awareness

Awareness requires attending, for without clear attention, awareness will remain immature. Our fish story demonstrates that awareness develops only when we place our attention and quiet our mind. This process can be uncomfortable at first, as we move through various stages of boredom and the perception that nothing is happening. A wise man once told to me to pay attention to boredom because it means something *is* happening and trying to come into consciousness. Boredom is a resistance to awareness. The mind will try to divert us by insisting our problem is that nothing interesting is occurring. But that is its nature— to maintain homeostasis and keep things from changing.

In Hindu philosophy this capacity is called *witness consciousness*. In the west we have called it the *observing self*. Whatever the name used, the idea is the same: clear, full and open attending with no judgment of or attachment to what is being perceived. A woman once described her experience of a deep state of witness consciousness:

I was sitting quietly, not really thinking of anything. Just being with myself and the beautiful trees around me. Very slowly a sense opened up that pervaded everything. I could feel a presence looking through my eyes. It was looking at itself because everything it saw was itself. There weren't words for this at the time. I had to translate the experience later. But this being, this consciousness was everything. Such a wonderful sense of peace that contained both stillness and pulsation!

While productive living in this world is greatly enhanced by turning this awareness toward one's life and activities, the deep spiritual journey begins with turning this awareness toward the source of that awareness. This is the path to God. A whole person is able to both live in this world effectively and connect with divinity. Awareness is a fundamental meta-tool for this endeavor.

Focus as the Second Prerequisite

Focus refers to the type of attention we bring to awareness. Using light as a metaphor, focus can be wide and global like a flood light, or narrow and tight like a laser light. Most people prefer one or the other type of focus. Each has its own capacities. A laser focus is good for illuminating details or identifying a specific target. A flood light focus is good for general scanning and searching over a wide area. The point is to be able to do both and match the type of focus to the task.

People who tend to use a laser focus will be very good with details. If they are not flexible with their focusing style, they will be the individuals who miss the forest for the trees. They can lose the main point as they tightly focus on the immediate concern. Conversely, a global focuser can be excellent at comprehending the overall picture of a situation and tend not to give enough attention to the particulars. Using the awareness exercises in this section will help correct imbalances created by style preference.

In addition to these two ways of focusing, there is a third: split-focus. This involves attending to two points of focus simultaneously. Split-focus is both an ability and a style of focus. The mother who is in the kitchen preparing dinner while she is listening and monitoring her children in the living room is utilizing split-focus. Here is basis for children's belief that "my mother has eyes in the back of her head".

Split-focus does not always serve a person well. Everyone has had the experience of talking to someone who clearly is focusing on something else besides the present conversation. Split-focusing does not lend itself to good conversational listening. Again, the point here is that when well applied this type of focusing is wonderful and when not, the result is preoccupation and non-attention.

The Observer and the Observed

In developing mature awareness, an important differentiation is made between the observer and what is being observed. This point may be obvious in a situation where a person is observing an elephant. Clearly the observer is not what is being observed. The situation usually does not remain so apparent when what is being observed by the person is his or her own anger or chronic negativity. There is a tendency to assume these aspects or feeling states are a natural and permanent part of the self. I have had people tell me they can't change a behavior or attitude because that's just who they are. The observer who is non-attached and non-judgmental would say—"No, these are experiences but they are not the same thing as the self." The Buddhist tradition uses a beautiful metaphor for this situation. We are said to be like the clear blue sky and all of our experiences are simply the clouds. Our task is to remember we are the sky and not the clouds.

The maturation process in the life journey seems to require the human to understand that one is not the body, not the emotions and not the thoughts. So an arm can be lost and that may be a very painful loss, but the person is still the person. Feelings may run the gamut from agony to bliss and the person is still the person. The mind may hold any number of thoughts and beliefs which can change or not, but the person is still the person. So who is left? The answer is found by turning the awareness back upon itself. This simple, yet fundamentally profound turning of awareness, initiates a deep awakening.

Ring of Awareness

People tend to set a "ring of awareness" around themselves and unless something unusual happens to cause a resetting, they monitor only what occurs within that ring. The size of this ring, which is usually set automatically and without conscious intent, varies with task, context and personal habit. For example, some drivers monitor the road only a few car lengths ahead and behind, while others scan as far as the eye can see in either direction. A driver using a large ring, however, will probably instantly contract that ring if the person directly in front of him suddenly slams on the breaks.

The area within any given ring doesn't always get equal attention. Again, usually through habit patterns, a person may tend to check the center of the ring more often than the edge or vice versa. A person may be more cognizant of what is happening in front and not so aware of what is occurring behind. These tendencies of attention play a large part in creating our perceived reality. An awareness pattern is neither right nor wrong. Some patterns are simply more effective in certain situations. In the driver example, the larger "ring of awareness" is a better match for the task. A driver who attends frequently to events directly behind will probably be able to monitor what the kids are doing in the back seat fairly well.

In very practical ways, identifying what our awareness patterns are and learning how to shift them for the specific situation we are in, expand our potential to live effectively in the world.

These exercises are designed to help you strengthen capacities that will aid you in your other processes. Remember you are working with a meta-tool and so in many ways doing these exercises are like the scales a singer practices. She is not really singing a song, but what she does will help her songs to be more beautiful and her singing more masterful.

Exercise # 14: Ring of Awareness

To do this exercise, read only through the three simple steps and then close your eyes.

1. Feel yourself. Take several breaths and be present to yourself.

2. Now feel your environment.

3. Open your eyes

Now begin to notice how you defined environment. Was it the few feet around you? Was it defined by the size of the room you are in? Did it include a space larger than that? The farthest edge you included in your awareness of your environment marks the size of your "ring of awareness" (for this moment in time.)

Now notice if you focused equally in the front or back of yourself. Did you "hold" the environment in your awareness globally, as a whole, or did you spot check it, training your focus first on one part and then on another?

Further practice: Begin to notice your "ring of awareness" as you go about your day. Once you have a good sense of your typical pattern, try altering it. For example, if you tend to hold a close focus, expand it or if your focus is broad, bring it in. If you rarely check your back, do so more frequently. Notice what you become aware of when you hold your attention differently.

Exercise # 15: Finding the Observer

1. Set your ring of awareness at a comfortable size.

2. Now with your awareness, locate the edge of your ring. This point is now the object of your attention.

3. *Notice where your awareness is coming from in your body. It will probably be either in your head, your chest or your belly. This point is the seat of your observer or witness. (If this exercise seems confusing to you and you want to say your head because you are looking with your physical eyes, try doing the steps with your eyes closed.)*

4. *Let the ring start shrinking, becoming smaller and smaller, until it is a dot inside your physical body. Where is the dot? Notice the distance between the dot and the seat of your observer.*

5. *Now let the observer move closer and closer to the dot and notice how that feels. Can you get the dot (that which is observed) to merge with the seat of your observer/witness? If you can, what do you experience when they are at the same point?*

Exercise # 16: Advanced Awareness

After you start working with your awareness, you will begin to find that there are many things that you can do with it. Once when I was in training to learn how to help people cleanse and detoxify their bodies, my teacher asked me to check on how the participants were doing. I was standing at a sink in the kitchen at the time and so I turned to leave the room. "No," she said, "Stay where you are." It was at this point I realized I could consciously decide to send my awareness out and scan any part of my environment. This phenomenon had been occurring spontaneously for quite some time but I never thought to use it consciously.

To begin working with this practice, use something that is an ordinary part of your day and that you can easily verify. Traffic patterns are a good place to start. Before you depart for your trip, establish your alignment and then imagine the route you are going to take. The image can be realistic or symbolic. You can imagine a real road or a line of energy. Now using your internal senses, scan along the route. Notice if it is clear or if there are blockages along the way. The point here is to relax and have nothing invested in your level of accuracy. Just check and notice what you find. The rest is simple. Take your trip and see how accurate you were.

Another place to practice is in restaurants. Put your alignment in place. Look at the menu and find what appeals to you. Now take your awareness into the kitchen and check those items out. How appealing are these items now? You can check for freshness and good preparation. Again, each person will have his or her unique cues. Since you are working with food, pay close attention to your stomach. You can determine how the food will sit before you eat it. This is a subtle practice. You don't have to be dramatic or obvious.

The idea here is to integrate this practice into your daily routine and to do it often enough that you can really hone your skills. Another way to say this is— only use these practices when you want to be effective and empowered and need to know what is going on in your life. This type of scanning is purposeful and conscious and not like the ongoing hypervigilant checking that can go on in the second chakra.

Over time you will begin to learn how to interpret what you are picking up. People have different ways of representing to themselves what they are sensing or seeing on the subtle levels. For one individual, light traffic might translate into a feeling of freedom and ease. For another, the information will come as a clear uninterrupted line of energy. Someone else might "just know". I have found that once you know how to place your awareness, the real learning becomes one of understanding and making sense of the information you are receiving. This knowing only comes with practice. I can tell you that since using this technique, I have been rarely surprised by traffic patterns and usually quite happy with my food choices in restaurants.

The Human Ego

What is the ego?

Since the ego so powerfully influences our perceptions, it can be very helpful to understand what it is and how it functions. The ego is a process-structure within the human system that is designed to mediate reality. At a

107

physical level it organizes our sense perceptions, integrates and interprets this information. For example, when you look out your window and see trees and grass and sky, all of this makes sense to you because your ego has already organized, categorized and filed this data from previous visual experiences. Just like the boy with the fish, you have the sense of knowing what you are looking at as you gaze at the scenery. Or more accurately, you think you do and for most practical purposes this assumption works.

At the physical level the ego functions out of a complex system of electrochemical processes. This process acts as a gate to keep consciousness contained and anchors it into a limited band of physical reality. This gate-keeping allows a person to attend to practical details of living and functioning in third dimensional reality. The ego mediates time and space in such a way that we can drive cars, ride bikes and rendezvous with people and places at appointed hours. One theory suggests that when a person takes a hallucinogenic drug, such as LSD, the ego is chemically stripped out of the system by dramatically lowering serotonin. The person then "trips" and experiences reality without the aid of an ego structure. If there is not a sufficient development of the inner witness, the results can be disastrous. In some tribes within the Native American culture the use of mind-altering substances, such as peyote, is part of religious practice. This practice is usually overseen by the presence of a teacher or shaman who is able to "lend" his or her healthy ego if needed. Psychologically, as part of the mind, the ego separates, compares, contrasts and classifies what it perceives against previously organized information. The ego thus determines states of me and not me, good and bad, true and untrue, apples and oranges, alive and not alive and so forth.

The Role of Ego, Identity and Awareness

By its nature the ego organizes perceptions and identifies with its experiences. For example, because I have a body, my ego says "I am this body." I also have thoughts and feelings which my ego is familiar with and will include this information in its definition of me. These identifications tend to become static structures by which other physical, emotional and cognitive experiences are compared. Additionally, there is a tendency for the ego to make a stronger identification with one level of self over another. People will say, "I'm such a physical person," or, "I'm a cerebral type," or, "I am all emotion," or, "I'm a spiritual person." They are communicating their level of identification because, in fact, each person is all four. These patterns of identity strongly influence perception and awareness.

Identity is simply a constellation of images and beliefs about who or what we think we are. Identity is mediated by the ego and by definition is limited because it is based on the assumption that we have certain qualities and that we do not have others. Humans learn and mature by moving through a series of identities, many of which revolve around the roles we play. We start with being a human baby, a girl or boy, a son or daughter, a student, a parent. Other parts of our identity come through feedback our parents and early caretakers give us: We are told we are generous, careless, responsible, selfish, good or bad.

Having an identity allows us to deeply explore smaller parts of ourselves without being overwhelmed with too many possibilities. Thus we are taught we are human and that we are not a horse or a cloud or a piece of furniture. Ideally this process allows for safe exploration and does not trap us in limitation. As the person matures, the individual moves on to new identities. Sometime an old one must end and a new one needs to be acquired. At other times an old identity is expanded into a larger definition of self. How a person navigates these shifts is very personal and unique to that individual.

There is no one correct way to shift an identity. I know a young man who absolutely had to face the end of his childhood. In order for him to be a successful father, he needed to end his sense of himself as a boy and take on the mantle and authority of his own manhood. I have also seen a woman grow into her next level of power by opening to the joy of her inner little girl and freeing this part of herself to express and create in the world.

When identities shift rapidly, the experience can be very painful if we are heavily invested in that particular identity. A woman I worked with once was devastated when her husband died. She not only felt the loss of her life companion; she felt as if she had lost herself. This woman, who had largely identified herself through her husband and his accomplishments, did not know who she was without him. Her grief process required her to not only address her sorrow but to also find a sense of herself that was not referenced to her mate. We must be willing to release what we have attached to or identified with in order to grow. What can make this letting go disorienting is that we are flung into the unknown, for identity carries not only a sense of who we are but it also gives us a notion of our place in the world.

The strong tendency to be aware only of what reinforces the present identity acts as a filter to self-perception. If Henry, for example, views himself as an honest man, then seeing where he is not honest tends to be difficult. He may tell himself that his lack of honesty in a particular situation is not important or is, in fact, smart. He may not even know of his own dishonesty. If on the other hand Jane does not see herself as creative, she will be blind to her own creative impulses. I once worked with a brilliant young musician. She won awards for her playing. She told me she really couldn't play the violin and maintained that when she performed, she was only faking. The ego's influence is that it causes us to see what we think is there and not what really exists.

By definition the ego processes through the past because it utilizes only what it has already experienced. Here is the conundrum: We need the ego to establish ourselves in physical reality and this same function can keep us stuck. *The strength of the ego is in its capacity to separate out patterns to enhance our learning experience and this function is also its great limitation.* The ego is designed to process data in a very specific manner. It does not appear to be designed to explore what is not already known. Therefore when faced with moving into the unknown, we must rely on other parts of ourselves. Fortunately, the heart is a great leaper. If she has faith and hope, she will go anywhere.

Spiritual traditions, especially those that embrace a rejection of the mundane world, have had a tendency to regard the ego as almost an enemy to be beaten back and subdued. Understanding the ego's role in our development as human beings can allow us to utilize the ego appropriately and not ask it to perform functions for which it was not designed. To be sure, it will tend to push its services forward but we can learn to decline its offer.

To counteract this limitation of the ego, we can embrace a love of mystery and cultivate wonderment. To celebrate the state of not knowing allows us to move into the unknown and become present. Only then can we slip from patterns of the past which threaten us with ongoing replication into the future. The true present has no history and hence is filled with creative potential. Albert Einstein was speaking to this truth when he talked about what he most valued in life: mystery and imagination.

Awareness, when properly practiced, allows for a healthy release of ego. The ego has been likened to the protective shell of a nut which has the function of protecting the nut meat while it is forming and maturing. When this protection is no longer needed, we can crack the nut so to speak and release the meat. By simply becoming aware of when the ego is identifying and reacting and calmly watching this occurrence, we weaken the hold the ego has on our perceptions. When is the ego reacting? When we feel superior, inferior, rejected, offended, incensed, righteous, overlooked, our ego is in reactive mode.

The ego's presence and influence over determining our perceptions can also operate at much more subtle levels. Many people cannot perceive subtle energy because the ego believes that level doesn't exist and has trained the person not to see, hear or feel this part of our world. We don't necessarily feel the ego exerting its influence in this case. When working with the ego, it's best to focus on the level that is more obvious, such as emotional reactivity. Over time you can address the ego with greater and greater discernment.

Exercise # 17: I Am That I Am Meditation

This purpose of this meditative exercise is to take you beyond your human definition of yourself and into a higher identity of Spirit. (Please read Chapter Five which covers the tenth, eleventh and twelfth chakras.)

Start with sitting comfortably. Close your eyes. (If you have not had a bowel movement or if you are a woman having on your period, then simply pick a spot on the floor, about two feet in front of you and keep your eyes open.) Take three long, deep belly breaths. Inhale through the nose and exhale very slowly through the mouth.

Establish your alignment and feel the light within your Core. As you focus on the light, use the phase I AM. Become the light that you are. You are shifting your identification to the soul, to your eternal Self. This I AM is the Christos in human form, the inner Buddha, the original Adamic, (as in Adam), Self. Feel this level as the real you. Establish this focus very strongly and hold for several minutes. Let this light pulsate. As this light undulates and streams, know that you are experiencing what the Hindus call Cosmic Consciousness.

From the light within your Core, feel the light that is everywhere around you. Know that this light inside of you and all round you is the same light. Let this experience become very vivid and strong. Using your awareness will strengthen this perception. Now use the phase, I AM THAT. Feel the words. Feel the consciousness that is behind these words. Breathe and pulsate with the light you are becoming. You are creating an alignment here with the Christos in God. Ride with your experience. Feel the pulsations. Enjoy the dance of light and your experience of Unity Consciousness.

Now you will take a leap. You are switching perspectives. The little self is dissolving. Before you were a point of light relating to all other points of light. Now you become I AM THAT I AM. You step into God. You become all of the light. You let go of all previous identifications. You are the One light that is all. Feel the pulsations, weaving back and forth throughout all of existence and beyond. This is God Consciousness. As you end your meditation, bring back your expanded Self. Repeat your three breaths, asking that your body, all the organs, each cell, adjust to the frequencies you are now carrying.

The Power of Awareness and Subtle Energetic Work

There are three principles that are very significant in understanding the power of awareness.

1. Awareness can change what it observes.
2. Awareness can direct energy.
3. Awareness cultivates the capacity for discernment.

Awareness can change what it observes. The degree of change will be influenced by the clarity of the awareness, the intention of the observer and the type of focus used. By using an awareness that is foundationed in compassion, one can bring transformation to what is being observed. Conversely, one can amplify a fear by placing awareness on it. The adage, "Don't put your mind on it, that will only make it worse," holds some truth. But ignoring such things as our fears can also cause them to operate out of our awareness or control. So the question becomes, how can I place awareness on a fear without increasing it? Here is where intention and type of focus come into play. By setting an intention to resolve or heal a fear, awareness is altered. Additionally, by using a split-focus and remaining aware of a consciousness of light or compassion, the dynamic is altered because the fear is being connected to a higher vibration.

Awareness directs energy. The act of placing our awareness on a point begins to draw energy to that area. This is true if the point exists in the physical body or if it is a point in consciousness. This principle is important to understand when dealing with consciousness because too much awareness placed on negativity can actually increase it. For example, when I am working with a negative pattern involving fear or anger in someone, if I do not split my focus and keep myself largely aware of divine consciousness, I can increase fear or anger by one of two ways: I can "grow" the negativity in the other person (it will appear to proliferate) or I can become so focused on the negativity that my own energetic system comes into resonance with the lower vibration. Note: Often as part of the healing process, repressed feelings will rise to the surface for release. This appearance of strong negative emotion is not the same thing as the proliferation of negativity.

Awareness cultivates the capacity for discernment. Through practicing conscious awareness we cultivate the capacity for discernment. Discernment implies a subtle and penetrating ability to differentiate and comprehend. Just as the indigenous Eskimos can discern more than a dozen types of snow simply because they have observed snow for so long, so can we increase discernment by simply using awareness. This skill seems to come gradually for most people. Years ago, I had been practicing "feeling" various objects, comparing silver to gold, diamonds to quartz and those types of things. At first I could only dimly sense a difference but with practice the qualities became quite distinct. One day my son and husband came back from a flea market and my four-year-old son gave me a ring he and his dad had purchased for 25 cents. I held the ring to see what I could sense and was surprised to feel a vibration I had felt earlier with diamonds. This ring seemed to me quite gaudy and cheap looking. My mother, who was with me at the time, had a good eye for stones. She said she didn't think it looked like diamonds but she was curious and took the ring to a jeweler. He confirmed that the stones were, in fact, diamonds. The reason they didn't look real was because they were faceted with an old-fashioned miners cut that was no longer used. Although this incident was fun and lucrative, discernment has many more practical applications. Selecting food in the grocery, choosing vitamins and personal products are ways to use discernment in one's everyday life to make more healthful choices. The ultimate use for discernment, however, is in dealing with important decisions we make in our lives and in navigating inner realities. Our growing awareness eventually becomes the light that illuminates our path. Awareness can be said to almost equal *awakeness*. More accurately, awareness that has birthed discernment creates the awakened.

Attention and the Body-Heart-Mind-Spirit

Attention can be placed anywhere on the physical, emotional, mental or spiritual levels of life. As humans we each have a tendency to have a preferred level. So some people will tend to be aware of the physical world and others will focus more on the emotional, intellectual or spiritual level. We choose careers or work based on these tendencies. Our perceptions of life and what we value also come out of these preferences. To a certain extent these preferences reflect our uniqueness. These tendencies can also create distortions and imbalances in our lives. As we bring awareness to our attention patterns, we can bring ourselves into greater balance which translates into better health, stronger clarity and peace.

Jennifer, a former client of mine, was a beautiful single young woman in her thirties. She was deeply spiritual and exceptionally intelligent. She actively devalued the physical level of life and saw all things physical as lesser in importance. Despite being in her thirties she had never worked. Money was not important. Her focus was in the world of ideas, philosophy and Spirit. Not surprisingly, her both her physical and psychological health were poor. She never gave herself the opportunity to learn or gain a sense of competence in dealing with everyday reality. Jennifer also did not value emotions and as a result did not deal with hers. Fears were skimmed over and not faced. Only Spirit and ideas mattered. Until she balances herself, the wonderful gifts she has will remain in the invisible worlds.

Ella, another woman I worked with, was also in her thirties. She was very focused on both the material and emotional world. Spirit frightened her and she was unsure of her intellectual capacities. She did choose to address her imbalances. She began to explore spirituality and used her mind to evaluate what she saw, read and experienced. Because her emotional self was nicely developed, she was able to use this part to help herself determine which path was right for her spiritually. Her life changed dramatically as she found meaningful life work and a more balanced place for the material aspect of her life.

Each person needs to access his or her state of development in these areas. By becoming aware of weaker levels and strengthening them, the power to create opens dramatically. Our spiritual level gives us vision and meaning. Our mind can map the vision. Our emotions and feelings provide the desire that is needed to pursue our vision or dream. The physical world is the workshop, the playground where the vision can come into form.

Humans are here to create—that is what we do. Humanity is creating our reality this very moment. Unfortunately many are manifesting their reality from imbalance, fear and ignorance. The question is *what* we create, not if. When we are balanced, when the ego does not dominate us and when we are awake and aware, we can create and manifest visions and dreams of incredible beauty and love. Awareness is your meta-tool for perceiving your path, discovering who you are and finding your potential.

Internalization of the Senses

In order to take the level of awareness into the realm of the subtle, we must internalize the senses. This means to withdraw the senses of touch, sight, sound, taste and smell from the physical world and place them on the subtle. Many of the exercises in this book are designed to help facilitate this shift. Meditation is also a powerful way to achieve this internalization. Just as the boy who looked at the fish saw more and more when he finally surrendered his awareness to the task, so can we begin to perceive profoundly when we practice with the eye on the subtle. This practice cultivates and develops our intuitive ability.

Chapter Eight

Intention as a Meta-Tool

Intention is considered to be a meta-tool because of the far reaching effects of its influence. Operating at both conscious and subconscious levels, intention is always in action. When there is a discrepancy between levels, what is being held in the subconscious will often hold sway. A teacher once said to me, "What you are unaware of has far more control over you than that which you know about." Self-honesty will take you far in your work with intentions. Learn to welcome those embarrassing moments of unflattering self-awareness. For when they happen, you are truly then in a position to do something about them. Many of us live with *survival* intentions without realizing what we are doing.

Survival intentions create survival lives. When we begin to step back and take a more expanded view of ourselves, one that includes the alignment of body, the psyche and the spirit, we can begin to live intentions that create *awakened,* lucid lives. This chapter reviews several aspects of this meta-tool: its function as a dynamic principle of creation and its use as a conscious healing and manifestation technique.

Intention as a Dynamic

Intention can operate as both a directive and a motive. An individual, for example, can intend to speak the truth at all times. This is the conscious, directive level of her intention. She may have any number of motives: to live her spiritual beliefs, to honor herself and others, to avoid getting caught for lying or to comply with the values of her family's tradition. Her motive reflects a deeper level of her intention because it reveals the state of consciousness from which she is functioning. For purposes of subtle energy work, this is a crucial point because what we create is strongly affected by the type of consciousness we hold in that process. The more the directive and motive aspects are coherent and congruent, the more powerful the effect of the intention. Another way to say this is that when we hold high levels of integrity, our capacity to heal and create increases dramatically. Integrity in this sense is used to mean *literal* integrity of the mind-body-spirit system. When the mind, the heart, the body and action are aligned, we move unimpeded by inner conflict. When one part of ourselves goes one way and the others go in different directions, we create energetic stalemates within our system. This principle applies whether the system is an individual or a group of people. The power of integrity and coherency can translate into speed when manifesting both healing and creativity.

The Issue of Motive and the 3-Brain Human

The motives that drive both our internal and external behaviors reveal our operating intentions which are not necessarily the same as our stated ones. One model of the human system proposes that we have three brains: a head brain, a heart brain and a gut brain. Within both the abdominal region and the heart area, the physical body contains the same type of tissue found in the brain, further suggesting that these three areas contain complex information processing centers. Many people in our society have learned to place less value on the heart and gut brains. In doing so, there is less conscious access to them but they are no less powerful in their influence.

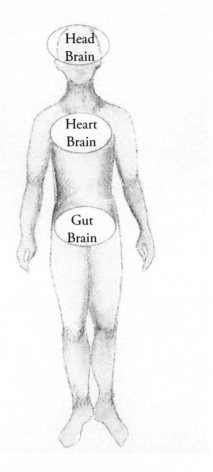

Illustration-15: The 3-Brain Human

The *head brain* thinks, analyzes, envisions and plans. Mystical systems call this part of ourselves the lower mind and egoic self. The *heart brain* feels, intuits and desires. The *gut brain* is instinctual, practical and concerns itself with the outer world and keeping us alive. One can say the head thinks, the heart feels and the gut acts. When they are cooperating and in sync, they are a dynamic team. When they are in a state of conflict they can leave us feeling as if we are caught in an inner filibuster. By over laying the chakra system model over this three-brain model, we can see that they correspond beautifully.

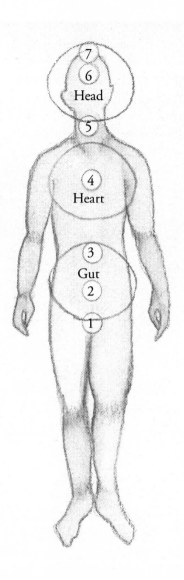

Illustration-16: Combining the 3-Brain Model with the Chakra System

Both models would suggest that in order to work with an intention we must be able to envision it, want it and be able to act on it. Lack of alignment or commitment from any of these three levels will net mixed or poorly sustained results. Consider the following situation: David's head says, "Eating healthy foods is a good idea. I want that as part of my life." His heart says, "But I give everything to everyone. The least I deserve is eating what I want." His gut says, "Nothing I ever do works." As long as these three are out of alignment, healthy eating will remain a good head idea.

Many people have tried unsuccessfully to achieve greater abundance in their lives. Intending abundance will only work if all three brains are engaged. *Creation requires vision, desire and action.* If there is unfocused action, guilt about abundance, feelings that money is dangerous or corrupting or the belief that the way life works is that one must struggle hard for little yield, this intention will just bring frustration.

Partnership with Self

What we come to as a means of achieving real coherency and congruency and hence effectiveness within ourselves is the notion of partnership. Partnership requires participation and cooperation, with each part contributing what it does best. Within a context of respect, all parts become equally valued because each gives something that is needed.

The head cannot feel or act. The gut does not envision a larger picture. The heart does not plan or analyze. Each of these parts of ourselves has been exquisitely designed to function in a particular way. When we ask these parts to come together and contribute what they have to give and not ask them to perform other functions, we gain clarity.

Additionally, to become deeply creative we must be willing to step into the unknown. We must be willing to tolerate a little chaos. The head (the lower mind and ego) does not go into these places easily. It is our heart, when it can feel right about the leap, that is willing to go. Yet this adventurous aspect of the heart needs the head and the gut to figure out the particulars. These three can be considered the human trinity. When your gut and head serve your heart, you have balance within this lower trinity.

Our three brains can tell us a lot about our motivations in life. Becoming clear about our motives is an important initial step when strengthening our capacity to use intention consciously.

Bringing the head, the heart and the gut into alignment and agreement creates a congruency and integrity in ourselves that empower us tremendously.

We become pure in our intent and powerful in our capacity to create and heal.

The Influence of Beliefs

We don't always create what we want. We create what we believe in most strongly. For this reason, becoming aware of our operating beliefs is extremely important. They form the ground of consciousness we stand upon and frame the window we look through to see reality. Many of our beliefs are inherited from our culture and our family. Part of the process of examining our motives and beliefs requires us to look at what we are carrying over from our families of origin. If you were given any beliefs that no longer serve the creation of a whole and loving life, it is your responsibility to shift them. They must leave your entire system—the physical body as well as your mind.

One of my teachers once said to me: "Have no beliefs." I was perplexed and unsettled by this statement. Weren't beliefs important? Didn't I have good ones? Could I lead a purposeful life without beliefs? This wise teacher was helping me see a very important truth: *Beliefs operate as intentions.* Most humans have both conscious and unconscious beliefs about just about everything: the state of the world, human nature, god nature, our bodies, our minds, our hearts, money, sex, work and play. The list is endless. We swim in a sea of beliefs and to the extent that we do, we cannot see clearly or know deeply.

Consider Sarah who believed she was a person who had suffered a lot of rejection in her life and believed she was unlovable as a result. Sarah did a simple life review of all the times she had felt rejection. She used her *awareness* to look at these events. Sarah reported that what she saw surprised her. She really hadn't been excessively rejected over the course of her lifetime. She did discover, however, a pattern of feeling very threatened by other people's anger. Sarah also was able to observe her tendency to personalize this anger and then interpret this as rejection. Sometimes she was rejected but it wasn't as often as she had previously thought. Interestingly, when her belief shifted, her feelings about herself changed and her level of self-confidence increased.

When you want to work consciously with intention, you must clear yourself of limiting beliefs. *Laying positive intentions over powerful negative beliefs is ineffective.* In some cases, it can escalate anxiety. Joanna, a woman who came to work with me, had stomach pains. Her doctor had checked her out and could find no evidence of disease. She ate a healthy diet. She had previously started using an intention, which was, "I release all stress from my stomach and live a full and happy life." Her stomach pains escalated dramatically and she began having panic attacks. It was at this point she contacted me. I asked her to tell me what her picture of a full and happy life was. She began to describe a very active work scenario and a full social agenda. As she spoke, it became clear to both of us that as good as this vision sounded, for her it was fraught with perils. She would lose control of her time and privacy. As we looked more closely at her operating beliefs, we found several: I have to please others and I have to work hard. Her stomach was not going to improve until she found other ways to set boundaries for herself and new beliefs that supported these behaviors.

Our belief structures function as seed bed for our reactive, less conscious intentions. For example the belief, "The world is unsafe," can be the foundation for a variety of reactive, defensive intentions:

I have to look out for # 1.
I have to sacrifice myself and my needs.
I have to fix it and make it better.
I have to get out of here.

Consider the impact of these commonly held negative beliefs:
People can't be trusted.
Things don't work out for me.
Humans will never change.
People with cancer die.
Healing takes time.

These types of beliefs affect not only the person who holds them. Remember we are part of the whole and what we hold affects all that is. Carl Jung once said that humans will not be able to create peace on this planet until enough of us have achieved this state within ourselves. Until that time, we will project our shadows onto the faces of others and call them the enemy. A person who hates himself, activates hatred in the world. Conversely, the person who loves himself, creates a greater love for all. I have often told people who are concerned with spending too much time on themselves and are afraid that this is selfish that when you work on inner peace, you work toward world peace.

Partnership with Spirit

As noted, the 3- Brain system represents the human component of our system. If our ability to create, learn and grow is going to match our real capacity, we must expand this model to include the Higher Self and Spirit. When we do, we become doorways into the world of Spirit, doorways that let us touch the invisible and doorways that let Spirit into the human world. Our model then looks like this:

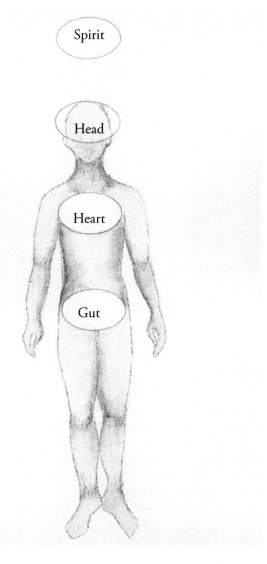

Illustration-17: Divine Partnership Model

123

The idea of co-creating with Spirit has been receiving more and more attention in recent years and is part of the emerging Unitive paradigm. We are beginning to understand that relating to the divine isn't a matter of being good children and asking in the right way for the goodies we want. Co-creating involves a respectful, personal partnership where we function as self-responsible adults. By learning how to keep our head, heart and gut in partnership we prepare ourselves for partnering with Spirit. This is not a linear process. To the extent we can be fair, honest and loving with ourselves, to that degree we can co-create with God. By showing up for ourselves and learning how to be non-judgmentally present, we begin to step upon the ground where we can have a mature relationship with our Higher Self, our soul and our God.

Intention as a Directive

When we are congruent and coherent within our system, intention begins to function as a powerful conscious directive. It acts as an index within the conscious, the subconscious and the subtle energetic levels. To use a computer metaphor, when we hold and state an intention, it is like we are typing in a file name to locate a particular part of the system. The computer in our case is the whole fabric of consciousness both within our immediate sphere and within all of creation. How can this be so? Remember we live in a holographic reality. Each person is connected to and is a reflection of the whole. Thus, our own system is an index to everything. How we get into the index is through intention. The clearer and more coherent the intention, the more powerful and effective it is. The system we may be accessing may be our own, another person's, a group of people, or the planet. The function of intention remains the same. If you have practiced any of the suggested energy exercises, then you will remember at a certain point you went into your cellular level. You did that through intention. To the lower mind which is so tuned to following things in a linear manner, this process may seem to be ridiculously simple. Please accept that it is that easy. With this wonderful meta-tool we can determine where we go within our target system, what we hold there and what we create. When we keep the Higher Self in the drivers seat, we keep the process safe for ourselves and others.

A number of years ago I underwent a lengthy medical procedure. As I waited to go into surgery, my mind listed all of the things that could go wrong. Needless to say this increased my anxiety and fear considerably. In one clear moment, I saw I had an opportunity to not only heal physically, but to shift a long-standing distrust of doctors. I called upon my "Zen Mind", the part of me that knew nothing and didn't have an investment in negative beliefs about the medical profession. I held the intention that the higher selves of *all* those involved come forth and guide each of us to be our most brilliant healing selves. I held that intention with love for us all. The surgery went beautifully. I received exquisite care and healed very quickly. I also had my first experience of feeling gratitude to the nurses and doctors. Every day we have opportunities to live richly through our conscious use of intention.

Intention as a Practice Tool

The Use of Words

Use the *present tense* when you state your intention. We create in the present, not the past or the future. To deeply understand this principle is both freeing and empowering. The whole point is to *become present to the present.* Wording can affect the intensity of your intention. Try the following exercise: State the different versions of the love intention listed below. Embody each of them as you repeat them three times. Pause for a moment and feel your body responses.

"I am loved."
"I am loving."
"My heart holds love."
"I receive the love of God."
"I am love itself."

Sometimes an intention is stated too strongly and can bring up fear and negativity. Intention can initiate purification or release. You can adjust your phrasing to help you find the wording that works best for you. Overtime you can increase the boldness and strength of your intention. Daily affirmations are a type of intention practice that can be very rich if they are worded appropriately and personally for you. When you create an intention of this type, find a statement that empowers, energizes and does not overwhelm you. "I am in a perfect state of health", may need to become "My body grows stronger and healthier each moment." "Today, I live my truth", may need to be "Today I learn to live my truth."

Using surprising word combinations can also help you create wonderful, freeing intentions:

"Today I live outrageous delight."
"I taste the juiciness of my soul."
"I live the thunder of my gentleness."
"I am God's Lover."

The Use of Will

As with awareness, the use of will must be clear and light. There should be no sense of forcing or pushing. The purpose of will is to choose, direct and focus and not to provide the energy or fuel for the experience. People with very strong wills can often get confused over this point. If there seems to be resistance, then stop. Become aware of what is happening and let go of any sense of trying.

This way of working requires a certain type letting go and non-attachment. Sometimes the desire itself is so great that we get in our own way. When I was in my late twenties, I discovered a lump in my breast. Of course the discovery was made on a late Friday evening of a three-day weekend. By Monday morning, I was convinced I had end-stage cancer. Over the next three months, after seeing my gynecologist, another physician, a radiologist and a surgeon, the consensus was that it was probably not cancer. The surgeon said my choices were to have an exam every three months for two years or go ahead and get the lump removed. Determined to do things the natural way, I chose the former option and began daily visualizations. I also compulsively checked my breast many times during the day. After six weeks, my anxiety level was off the charts. All I thought about was my breast. Reluctantly, I decided to schedule surgery, since I did not seem to be in very good control of my mind. I was also very disappointed that my visualizations had done nothing. The nurse gave me an appointment for two weeks later. I stopped my imagery and stopped checking my breast. Knowing this was going to be taken care of, I let everything go.

When the surgeon examined me on the day of my appointment, he could not find the lump. I checked and I could not find it either. Certain that I was not locating it because of nervousness, I asked his assistant to feel for the lump too. Gone. I left the hospital baffled. Only later did I realize that I was like the person who wrote the letter but never mailed it. The desire and focus were there but I was holding on and trying too hard. Only after I had "given up" could my intention work.

The Role of Your Body

Your body can tell you if you need to adjust your intentions or affirmations. If the phrasing quickens and enlivens you, then your body is giving you an okay. If you feel nothing, then your body may be telling you that you are not connected to the intention or present in some way. Check to see if you are being really present and sincere. If you are, then this intention simply may not be important to work with right now. If you get a strong negative reaction, then you know you need to change the phrasing or investigate an underlying issue.

The Role of Your Heart

The head can help design an intention, the will can help you focus, but it is the heart that makes an intention go. The heart provides the fuel to energize the process. Think of a pot of soup on the stove. To make soup you need a pot, certain ingredients and fire. Your heart can provide that fire. If you have difficulty hearing your heart, you may want to begin to talk with it more often. Before sleep, check in to listen to its perspective of the day you have just lived. Greet it in the morning. The heart becomes quiet and sad when it is ignored. Our culture refers to this state as depression. By maintaining a good relationship with your heart, you will find a ready and eager partner in your healing and creating endeavors.

The Ethics of Intention

What if the Intention Doesn't Work?

If you are working with an intention that doesn't seem to be yielding results, several dynamics may be at work: 1) You may need to clear negative patterns, beliefs or feelings before the intention can take hold. 2) You may be trying too hard or using too much will which can actually prevent the intention from working. 3) You may not be truly sincere within your own heart. 4) Divinity may be at work.

If we are truly in partnership with Spirit and our intention is not coming together, there is a reason. We do not always know that reason. Showing up for our life in each moment and doing our best is all we are required to do. When we accept the results and move on, we put ourselves in the best position to live in happiness.

The Safety Clause: Thy Will Be Done

In any healing and manifestation work, we need to stay within the evolutionary parameters of Divine Will. This is what the prayer, "Thy will be done," achieves. In other words, this prayer provides a safety net because we can never know the entire workings of Spirit. Developing a strong connection to the eighth center helps to increase the capacity to hear higher guidance, but even those who have profoundly secured this connection will not always be able to hear and know Divinity's plan. Sometimes an illness is in fact the healing. Sometimes it is only needless suffering. Letting Higher Will work through us always assures us that we are not interfering with something larger than we currently understand.

Intentions for Others

When you are working with intentions for world peace, healing others, welfare of family and friends, remember that these intentions are entering a system where other agendas already exist.

I believe that the most masterful way to use intention is to not impose one's will on anyone else. *Create the intention in your own system and become a point of resonance and light for others.* Also, remember to work within your own evolutionary parameters, which is the context of God's will. Your intentions and consciousness are vitally important. We will have world peace when the larger system reaches a critical mass that flips humanity out of a fear-based reality into one that is based on peace and love. You have no way of knowing if you are going to be the one who tips the scale of the critical mass or not. You are not responsible for holding intentions *out there*. Hold the intention inside of yourself for your system and ask, intend, that what you hold and represent be gifted to all that is. Your God Self does all the rest. Intention is a wonderful and necessary meta-tool for self-mastery. The wise and apt use of this tool makes life much easier and free flowing. When we remember to work in partnership with ourselves, we don't get in our own way. When we remember to bring this partnership to God, we find grace.

Chapter Nine

Finding Paths to Wholeness

Healing is the recovery of our innate wholeness and serves the larger purpose of allowing a deeper realization of our creative potential. The question becomes, how do we find this wholeness and more effectively support our creativity? This section gives some additional ways to understand your journey and methods to aid you.

First, it is important to remember that most of us are extricating ourselves from past-conditioned responses, attitudes and beliefs, all of which keep us asleep and unavailable to the present moment. These repetitive cycles are often so familiar that they feel natural. We can come to expect struggle, failure, rejection and conflict as inevitable as we proceed on "autopilot". The present, however, has not been set or predetermined for it has not been lived. Whenever you begin to feel that you know exactly what is going to come next, you have a sure sign that you are recreating the past. Even in situations which have been initiated in the past that are unfolding rapidly, such as the last moments of a terminal cancer patient's life, or seconds before a car accident, the present moment still has room for change to occur even if only in how the experience is being felt. As humans we may not always determine exactly *what* we experience but as spiritual beings we have the innate ability to determine *how* we will experience the event. This capacity is a source of true power.

Many people live with such limited images of themselves and the world: The world is unsafe; People can't be trusted; I am not capable; Life is a struggle;

I am not lovable or worthy. These images are based on conclusions drawn from narrow moments in time or come from what others have said, done or believed. Imagine what it would be like if these same people saw those images for what they were— just pictures and stories—not truth. To use a metaphor from pop culture, anyone who is trying to wake up is in the position of Keanu Reeves in <u>The Matrix</u>. He must unplug from the illusion that has been passing itself off as life and then he must figure out if he is the one.

Exercises for Resolving the Past and Coming into the Present

As already stated, most of us live largely in and through the past. We may appear to be in the current moment but we are often using the filters of decisions and coping systems we created in childhood. Typically these lenses will be even more potent if the situation is emotionally charged. These filters were either given to us by our parents and early caretakers or they were ones we adopted to "manage" these people. Children can be brilliant in how they devise ways to deal with the families who raise them. How you chose to handle the dynamics of your childhood was probably quite creative. What you most need to know is that these coping strategies will tend to limit you now. This fact is not always emotionally obvious to us.

The other way we tie ourselves to the past is by literally leaving energetic parts of ourselves here and there along the journey. Any situation from the past that is still carrying a negative emotional charge when you remember it, is a sign that you have left yourself in the past. This part of you is not available to be here in the present.

We do not have to scour for every speck of unfinished business but we do have to clean enough of it out so that the negative complexes that are constellated in our systems can collapse. We also have to make room for the incredible fullness of our own essence. Think of it as housecleaning for the most beloved guest you can imagine. Only the guest is not really a guest at all. It is your real Self.

It is important to remember that we carry familial and cultural beliefs about healing: how long healing takes, what is possible to heal and what is not, what can heal us and what cannot.

Take a moment to reflect on your beliefs and attitudes about healing. Sometimes it is our beliefs about the nature of healing itself that block us. My story about the lump in my breast clearly shows that although at one level I was committed to alternative healing therapies, at another level my fears and beliefs required that I use more conventional methods to help myself. Each of us must, above all else, be honest with where we are in consciousness. By starting where we are, we can move forward.

Helpful hint: The more comfortable and safe you feel when you do these exercises, the more profound their effect will be.

Exercise # 18: Calling Yourself Home

Sit or lie down comfortably and close your eyes. Begin by taking three, very slow belly breaths. Try not to move your shoulders. With each in-breath, imagine you are bringing in fresh vital energy. With each out breath, imagine you are breathing out any fatigue or toxicity you are holding. Continue breathing gently, allowing the body to soften and become heavy. Some parts of you will do this more quickly than others. That's okay. Let yourself adopt an attitude of relaxed curiosity. The way you work at this level of yourself is to allow. Never push. Become aware of the parts of you that are contracted. Gently begin to breathe into these parts, letting yourself expand. Notice your reaction to this expansion. The key to these exercises is to notice with neutrality. No analyzing or interpreting. If you have a mind that likes to do those sorts of things, just tell it "Later," and return to your breath.

Once you have allowed yourself to deeply relax, begin to imagine that on the top of your head is a large beacon that is slowly turning in a 360-degree rotation. The light from this beacon shines out a very long way. It shines out across the planet and beyond. The beam is calibrated and set for your life force and only that. It is scanning across time and space for all the bits and pieces of you that you have left behind as you have gone through your life and your nighttime dreams. Begin to notice in any way your system gives you this information, what the beam is picking up. If you choose, you can also set the beam to include other lifetimes. When you are ready, ask the beacon to activate itself and draw back those parts of yourself that you have lost. Let the beacon become a powerful magnet that is set for your energy. Use your in breath and the beam to bring your self home. Feel your life force pour back into you. Notice where it goes in your body.

What does this feel like, to have you return to you? Breathe and expand the sensation. Ask your cells to receive the vitality of this life force. If there are parts of you that draw close but do not enter your body, that is okay. Accept the parts that are ready. Thank them. Thank yourself for having found them.

Breathe and ask your system to integrate this return at all levels– physically, emotionally, mentally and spiritually. Feel your body, how your breath moves you. Move your fingers and toes. When you are ready to open your eyes, do so slowly and gently. Explore the place you are in with your eyes, looking out from deep within. How does the world around you look and feel, now that you have more of yourself to experience it?

Exercise # 19: The Corridor of the Past

This exercise is designed so that you may use it over and over again to resolve and release the past. It is important to remember that the corridor in this imagery is in your psyche. All of the territory you explore is yours. So for example, if you are speaking with your mother, then you need to know that this is your mother as she operates in your psyche. It is the people who behave badly in our psyches that are the real problems.

This exercise involves a dialoguing process. Whenever you use internal dialogue there are several points to remember. First, this process is safe. You will only see, hear and discover what is appropriate for you at any given time. If at any time things feel too scary, you always have the option of opening your eyes. However, if you have a history of abuse and this exercise is upsetting to you, you may want to work with a therapist for this part of your clearing.

Second, when you speak to these various "characters," be clear, firm and respectful. The ones that you interview are as complex as any person you would meet in the outer world. Sometimes they will be exactly as they appear. Sometimes they will not. Bring your inner psychologist along with you to know the difference. If you suspect that your "character" is not being honest, then say so. Sometimes the answers you are given may be cryptic. You have the right to ask for clarification. Third, you will be working with a guide and so you will always have a resource with you. Ask for guidance and suggestions if you have the need. Fourth, remember that all parts of you are in their own process of growth and transformation. They are there for a reason. You may be called to let them go or you may be asked to facilitate their transformation. Your goal is to possess your self. Let the process determine how that happens. Fifth, each person has his or her own way of internal perception. You may see your images or feel them. You may hear words or simply sense what is being said. Don't worry about how you get the information at this point. Lastly, journaling these dialoguing exercises is generally very beneficial and helps you to integrate your experiences.

Beginning with the breathing and relaxation practice detailed in the Calling Yourself Home exercise. Use your breath to take yourself into inner space. Once you have turned your awareness inside, begin to imagine you are standing in a hallway. Notice the lighting, the walls, the floor and the colors around you. At the end of the hallway is a passageway that leads to a set of stairs. You walk through this passage and look at the stairs. There are ten of them. Count the steps as you use them. If your stairs go up, feel you self going up as you climb them. If your stairs go down, feel yourself going down as you descend. As you step off of the last stair, notice that ahead of you is a door. This door leads to the Corridor of the Past. Open the door and step through, closing the door behind you.

Take a moment to study the corridor. There are doors on both the right and left sides. Each door has a sign on it, naming the person, place or situation from the past. On the wall is a buzzer. Use it to call your guide. Let your guide assume its own form, which may be human, animal or light being. Know that everyone has a guide. No one is expected to maneuver this journey alone.

Your guide enters. Notice the form that your guide takes today. Greet each other. You now have a choice as how to proceed. You may simply walk down the Corridor and let the door choose you. It will signal you in some way. Or you may have already selected someone with whom you want to speak. Make your choice and find your door now.

Standing in front of your door, notice the color and material it is made from. Notice exactly what the sign says. Placing your hand on the handle or knob, turn it and let yourself in. You and your guide enter, closing the door behind you. What is here? Is this an inside place or an outside place? What is the lighting like? If it is dark, your guide will give you a lantern or show you where the light switch is. Who is waiting to see you? What form does this one take? What are you feeling right now?

You can begin your dialogue by saying, "It's time we speak." Notice the other's reaction to your words. This is the time to speak honestly and clearly about what is in your heart. Express your feelings frankly: What has hurt you, humiliated you, angered you, frightened you. (If you tend to get stuck in a particular feeling, make sure you are not avoiding some of the other emotion). Tell about what was lost or what was wanted and never received.

Let the other respond. If this one is not being straight with you, say so. Listen again. When everything that needs to be said has been spoken, bring your light beacon in and shine it on the other. Bring your life force back. Use your breath. Declare that you are reclaiming your power and your life force. Repeat this phrase as many times as you need to say it. Speak with conviction. Receive yourself, breathe, receive yourself.

Feel your body. Feel your heart. You are at another threshold: the threshold of forgiveness. The deepest forgiveness comes from the place of our wholeness, the place within us that knows our essence was not diminished, could never be diminished by another. If you are ready to forgive or try to forgive, go on to this next part. If not, it is okay. One day you will be ready. You have your life force. Release the other to the Divine, who will take care of the learning and the healing of this one. Declare this release and feel what happens in your own body.

If you have chosen to pass through the threshold of forgiveness then know this: Your first forgiveness is of you. You may not feel that there is anything in yourself to forgive. Perhaps you feel it was entirely the other's fault. But sometimes a part of us can be angry with ourselves for even having the experience at all. So try the words, "I claim my wholeness and forgive myself." Let your body tell you whether or not you need self-forgiveness. Breathe and ask for the quality of forgiveness to open in your heart. If there is reluctance, know there is a fear here. Look at the fear gently. Feel your wholeness. Breathe. Ask again to experience the quality of forgiveness.

When you are ready, turn to the other and extend that forgiveness. Know that you are not saying you condone what has happened. In the end, forgiveness is the remembrance of wholeness. Breathe. Feel your wholeness. Your spirit has returned home to you. Rejoice in that homecoming.

Release the other into Divine light, so that journey for this one may continue and that the learning and healing may come. Your guide turns to you and gives you a message that will help you with this part of your healing. Take that message in. Breathe. There is time for you to absorb what has happened.

When you are ready, you leave with your guide. You go through the door where you came in, closing it behind you. For a moment you turn and look at the door. Has it changed in any way? As you stand in the corridor, you thank your guide. Take a moment to thank your own heart because what you have done takes courage. You walk back to the stairs and as you use them, count from ten to one. Move back into the first hallway and begin to bring yourself back to your physical surroundings. Listen for the sounds around you. Feel your body. Wiggle your toes and fingers. Open your eyes.

Exercise # 20: Returning Energy to Where It Belongs

This exercise is very helpful in clearing and balancing yourself when there has been an inappropriate exchange between you and another person. When we are not able to strongly hold our center, we will tend to give our power away to others. This leak isn't just psychological. It is an energetic event. When our personal energy is placed outside of ourselves, we become tired, confused and weakened. Our personal energy belongs inside of us.

We are each designed to take in universal energy, which is limitless, and integrate this force into our own systems. Using other people's energy muddies the waters so to speak because it contains their vibrational signatures. Everyone has issues and those issues are reflected at the level of personal energy. So it makes sense that we source from a place that is limitless and basically clean—the universe itself.

Inappropriate energetic exchanges can go both ways. Some people can drain us, literally, of our life force. They are easy to spot because you feel tired, weak or powerless after being with them. Conversely we can take energy from other people because we are not adequately sourcing for ourselves. For example when we are overly seeking approval from others, we leak energetically and can drain those around us. Picking up or absorbing other people's energy is not in our best interest. When we feel undue pressure from expectations of another person, we can be absorbing their projections energetically. Whenever control issues are present, it is a good indication that unhealthy energetic exchanges are taking place. The following simple exercise will help you return all energies to where they belong.

Begin with making yourself comfortable. Close your eyes and turn your awareness inside. Use your three cleansing breaths to center. When you are ready, imagine the person you are going to clear with is in front of you, standing about six feet away. In front of each of you is a large donut-shaped magnet that is hanging in the air at the level of the solar plexus. Your magnet is set for only your personal energy. The other person's magnet is set for only his or her personal energy.

Your magnet now turns on and activates. It begins to glow a bright orange- gold. Perhaps you can even hear a slight humming sound. Relax your body and focus on your breath. Very gently now the magnet begins to draw out any of your energy that has found its way into the other person. Your energy streams into the magnet where it is cleared and then into you. Breathe and receive. Fill with your self. Your magnet will automatically turn off when the transmission is complete. Just notice how much energy moved in this direction.

Now the other person's magnet activates and turns on. This magnet too becomes a bright orange-gold color. Again, relax your body and breathe. Anything that you have picked up will begin to be drawn away back to the other person. How does it feel to be relieved of this energy? Breathe. Let the magnet do the work. Once again, when the process is complete, the magnet will turn itself off. Notice how much energy moved in this direction.

What does it feel like to be cleared and balanced? What does it feel like to be with the other person in this state? Just notice. Dissolve the image and bring your awareness back into your physical setting. Open your eyes.

Finding Wholeness

For the greatest healing and growth to occur, four concerns must be addressed: balance, choice, focus and partnership. In other words, we must achieve relative balance within the four-levels of self which were delineated in the holistic model, we must be free to choose what we want to live and create, we must be able to focus sufficiently to realize this end and lastly, we must know how to work in partnership with our greater Self and the greater whole. This section explores these concerns as they apply to the four-levels of being. In addition, we will see that just as the archetypes have faces of light and shadow, so do these four-levels of being.

The Physical Body as a Trap

In the A.A. recovery program there is a saying, "Never let yourself become too tired, hungry, angry or lonely". This is sage advice not only for the recovering addict who needs to keep herself as strong and alert as possible in order to stay sober, but is wise advice for anyone who is trying to change personal habits. When we take good care of our body, we are clearer and more able to meet our experiences without being thrown off balance. Spiritual traditions which emphasize healthy living habits reflect this principle. Traditions that recommend periodic fasting and internal cleansing recognize that a body filled with toxins can interfere with spiritual growth. When we are physically toxic, we are vibrationally denser. In Chinese Medicine, when the liver is sluggish or unclean, the practitioner knows that there will be problems with anger or the ability to make decisions clearly. A clean body supports a clear mind which in turn supports a calm heart.

The body can become a trap where we are caught in the thickness of our own physical form. We develop attachments or addictions that ultimately limit our experience. Addictions come in many forms. Substance addictions are the more obvious ones, but sex, gambling, shopping, T.V., computer games, reading and even thinking can all be addictions. They rob us of our capacity to live lives based on free choice because we are driven by compulsions. Addictions usually start as a way to self-comfort but they ultimately become a way of escaping life.

The Body as Ally

Many traditions have taught that the body is bad or that "the flesh is weak". I believe this perspective is a misinterpretation. Over identification and imbalance are more accurately the problems. When we over identify, we confuse ourselves into thinking that we are the body and then physical issues take on overwhelming and compelling proportions. The body has appetites for food, sex, rest, stimulation. An imbalance is created when we either overly focus on the physical or we ignore it. The interesting thing about imbalance is that it feeds greater imbalance. Conversely balance will try to sustain itself. Another way of saying this is that although balance may initially be difficult to create, maintaining it once it has been established is easier.

The physical body is an incredible gift of nature and until we really know that we will never fully open our first chakra and be at ease in our body. Shyam Bhatnager, a sound master from India, teaches that one of the abilities within the first center is the capacity to overcome both the fear of abandonment and death itself. There is no coincidence that the ability to master the earth realm is housed in the earth chakra itself.

Imagine for a moment that you were given an amazing organically intelligent spacesuit to wear, one that was designed to take you into an environment you normally couldn't inhabit. This spacesuit was engineered to perceive, monitor and interact with this environment in such a way that the more you interacted with the suit, the more information it gave you. It was not a mechanical inanimate object as much as a living organic and aware material which had the capacity to repair itself when given appropriate care.

Now know that if you are reading these words, you have already been given not a space suit but an Earth suit. You have called it your physical body.

The body was meant to anchor us and provide us with the capacity to perceive and explore physical reality. This gift was never meant to bog us down. The path to balancing this level of ourselves lies with appropriate care for our bodies and working with our addictions. Healthy diet, exercise, fresh air and good sleep patterns are all parts of this good care.

A word about addictions: First, everyone has some type of addiction. Second, dealing with this issue is hard and it is a process, but the return for effort is tremendous. Overcoming addictions has in my experience in working with people for 25 years, led to the most significant changes in terms of self-empowerment, self-awareness, self-love and growth. To take a stand with our addictions means that we have stopped running away from our selves and our lives.

Emotions as a Trap

The pattern that drives the greatest difficulty with respect to balance and the emotions is reactivity. When we are reacting, we are not creating or choosing. We are forgetting that we are not what we are experiencing. Some people have very easy access to their feelings and emotions and some do not. The tasks for these two types of people are somewhat different. For the emotionally based person, the first key to balance is finding appropriate modes of expressing these emotions. For the individual who is fairly unemotional, the first key is to identify feeling states. Everyone has emotions and it is important to note again that it is the emotions which we are least aware of that have the greatest potential to control us. Both types of people must master lowering reactivity and increasing the capacity to respond. Growing in this way, strengthens the inner witness tremendously. Witness consciousness is essential for spiritual growth because it has the capacity to penetrate illusion and falsehood.

The emotional arena has traditionally been the domain of psychotherapy. Duan Roth, a psychiatrist I once knew, would also add that the arts were here to help us emotionally integrate long before psychotherapy was around. He was right. As our culture has less actively engaged in the arts, we have seen a rise in the practice of psychotherapy. Perhaps this is not a coincidence. The creative arts help us express and balance emotions so that they do not sit as blocked energy in our system. Self expression helps bring the second chakra into balance.

When we are trapped by our reactivity, we are at the whim of anyone who pushes our buttons. We are not free to choose our actions and our words. Others set the pace for us and we are caught in an unending roller coaster of dramas and stories. If we avoid this drama by cutting off our emotions, then we lead frozen, sterile lives and we still are faced with emotions as our trap.

Emotions as a Source of Energy

Water is a universal symbol of feelings and emotions and for good reason. Both allow for fluidity and flow. Emotions and feeling can help us move. They are a source of energy. Balance in this level of ourselves allows us to use our emotions appropriately. In India, there is a powerful goddess named Durga who is often depicted riding a tiger. The tiger she rides is said to represent negativity. She has tamed this creature, however, and now it takes her where she wants to go. She uses this primitive energy source as fuel.

Candy Lightner is the mother of a twelve-year-old girl who was killed in an accident by a drunk driver. She has talked about how her grief and rage almost consumed her until she decided to channel this incredible level of feeling into something productive. She is the person most identified with MADD (Mothers Against Drunk Drivers) and for eight years headed this group. The members of this organization have worked successfully to have legislation put in place that reflects a stronger stance against drunk driving. Candy Lightner is a beautiful and inspiring example of someone who has taken a powerful emotion that could have ruined her life and used it to fuel an effort to change the world.

Thich Nhat Hanh, a Buddhist monk who is also a social activist, uses the metaphor of compost for negative emotion. He says our negativity is our garbage. As a good gardener he knows that composting the manure and kitchen scraps can turn garbage into "black gold," that wonderful soil which in turn can be used to grow glorious flowers and an abundance of vegetables. Fresh manure kills things. So does our unprocessed and unexamined garbage when we fling it out onto others in the form of defensive retorts and attacks. Composted, manure produces incredible growth in the plants it nourishes. Once we are not reactive, we can sit and process our raw emotions, our

141

"garbage" and harvest the gold. That gold may be vital information we need to share to create a life-changing organization, a more honest and healthy relationship or a new direction in life.

Exercises for Creating Emotional Balance

Using the expressive arts is a safe and wonderful way to channel powerful emotions. By taking strong emotions and opening them up through a safe structure, we can meet and honor them respectfully. The most important thing I have discovered about feelings is that they need to be acknowledged and heard. Sometimes this act alone is enough to help us let go. When we work with our emotions by expressing them, a transformation often takes place. If we listen deeply and do not judge, the act of transferring feelings from inside ourselves to the outside in the form of words, colors, sound or movement changes our relationship to them. Insight is often gained by this process and we may discover for example, that the great anger we are feeling is sitting on a foundation of fear or that a sadness is not really sorrow but a frozen rage. As mentioned earlier, feeling can be likened to water. Strong feelings that have been held in can be thought of as a big river that has been dammed up. If there is no place to channel the water, releasing the dam is not wise. Expressive exercises provide a place to direct the flow, which can then free up life-giving energy. Matching the level of emotion to the expression is important. If, for example, you are feeling rage then journaling probably would not work. Journaling just lets one word out at a time. Something with large movements or big sounds is more in order. Working with Mandala art seems to fit a large range of emotions and levels of intensity. You have the advantage of being able to release and you have a recording of that release which may be helpful to contemplate.

Exercise # 21: Creating a Mandala

You will need some large paper and crayons, magic markers or pastel chalk. Mandala simply means circle. To create a Mandala, take a piece of paper and using a pencil, draw a big circle. You can use a bowl or dinner plate and trace around it. Sit with your paper and notice what emotion you are feeling and how strongly you are feeling it. Where is it in your body? Now look at the crayons or magic markers and sense which colors are catching your attention right now. Which colors seem to match what you are feeling? This is a neck-down process so don't use your mind to select your colors. Start putting the colors on the paper. The circle is only a reference point. You can stay in the circle or go out as you feel compelled. Use free-form lines or geometric shapes. Do not draw a specific picture of anything such as a tree or duck. Use shape, color and lines. When you are finished with one color, notice if you need to use another color. Your feelings will tell you what to put in and how much. They will also tell you when the Mandala is finished. When it is, recheck yourself. Has the emotion or intensity level shifted? Notice your body. Does your body feel different and if so how? Now try another Mandala, expressing where you are at this moment. You can use this process to peel yourself down like an onion until you find a place of stillness and peace.

Exercise # 22: Meeting the Inner Aspects

Note: This exercise involves meeting inner aspects of the self and becoming more conscious of them. If you want to learn more about this process, there are two reading sources that contain excellent material: <u>Psychosynthesis</u>, by Roberto Assagioli and <u>Embracing Our Selves: The Voice Dialogue Manual</u>, by Hal and Sidra Stone.

Before you begin, chose a part of yourself that you would like to explore. This aspect may have to do with your emotions, such as your angry self or your fearful self, or it may be some other part of you. Perhaps it is your caring self, or your artist self. The following is a structure that you can use to interview and dialogue with in order to better know yourself and your motivations. Some people find it helpful to have a notebook handy to record their dialoguing session. In many ways this process is like a waking dream. You have the advantage of being able to open your eyes at any time if the content becomes too upsetting. Try not to analyze the material as it comes up because this left brain activity tends to close down the imagery process. There is plenty of time to think after the experience. Remember that all parts of you are in their own process of transformation and growth. Your task is to become a good community leader that effectively utilizes and appropriately supports the development and healing of each community member.

Inside each of us is a cast of characters or inner community. In addition, we all have an internal social psychologist who studies and assesses people. Bring your psychologist with you on this journey. In this process as in all of life, some things are just as they appear and some are not. Some people are self aware and tell the truth. Some people do not understand themselves at all and cannot tell the truth. Inside of you are both types.

Exercise: Begin by closing your eyes and taking three cleansing breaths. Activate your alignment to enhance your clarity. Imagine now that you are walking down a hallway to a door which has a plaque with the name of your aspect. As you approach become very aware of the details of the door. What material is it made of? What color is it? Imagine the handle or knob vividly. Then placing your hand on the handle or knob, turn it and let yourself in. You step through the doorway and close the door behind you. Take a moment to orient yourself. What are you perceiving? What kind of place is this? What form does this aspect take? If it looks like you or someone you know, ask it to reconfigure itself. Introduce yourself and tell this aspect you have come to have a talk. Notice the response to your words. What is your sense of how this one is reacting to you? Are you welcome here? Do you feel the other trusts you? Just notice. Your task is to establish rapport with this aspect.

Ask this one how things have been going. How has it been for this one to live with you and the way you run things? Again notice the response. If the aspect is non-communicative, then simply start with describing your feelings about him or her. Ask if there is something that this one wants you to know? Or if there is something that this aspect wants from or for you. Use your psychologist and sense if this one is being straight with you. If you sense any falseness, you can simply say so. You have a right to be here and ask these questions. Be firm and respectful. Take time now to listen and to speak the things that need to be said.

When it is time to go, you reach into your pocket and pull out a gift to give. What is it? The one you have come to talk with also has a gift for you. What is it? Take a moment to dialogue with the gift, for it is a teacher and has a message for you. You say good-bye. Know that you can come back if you need to continue this discussion. You let yourself out of the room and close the door behind you. Once it is shut, look at the door again. Has it changed in anyway? Begin to focus on your breathing, bringing yourself back. Tell yourself you will count to three and when you open your eyes, you will feel refreshed, alert and calm. Now count to three and open your eyes.

The Mind as Tyrant

Western culture has elevated the intellect to a supreme position and as westerners we highly value the competent use and development of critical thinking and sound logic. Reason is often seen as the pinnacle of human development. To be sure, the technological achievements of our civilization would not be possible without this emphasis. The mind is a level of being within each of us, but our culturally biased values have added to its tendency to dominate our sense of who we are.

There is a famous teaching tale of the master who puts his servant butler in charge of the estate while the master goes on an extended trip. The master is gone for so long that the butler begins to believe that he himself is in fact the master. He runs the estate accordingly and is shocked when one day the master returns. This story speaks perfectly to the confusion that the mind makes concerning who is really running the show. The mind wants to believe that it is in control, in charge and creating everything that is happening. We do not have to look very far into ourselves to see this tendency. Our control issues are a reflection of this propensity. Freud's understanding of the ego/ mind was actually quite accurate, for he saw the egoic mind as being in a constant state of battle, trying to organize reality into some palatable form. Freud saw that distortion and blindness were readily and regularly used by the ego/mind to help create a more comfortable psychological world. This comfort however always comes at a high price and is never long lasting.

The mind is not bad. We have simply asked it to do things for which it was not designed. The intellect is very good at categorizing, labeling, comparing and searching for patterns. By definition the mind must work with the past because it can only analyze what it has already experienced. As the mind gathers data, it creates its own data base. From this base spring beliefs, attitudes and strongly held opinions which act as filters through which all new experiences are processed. The mind works through the process of identifying. The paradox is that identifying is part of how we learn new things but over time this same tendency will actually interfere with learning. Learning theory has called this influence 'prior learning interference', which simply means that once we have learned something one way, it is more difficult to learn it another.

The Zen practice of using beginner's mind is a very powerful way to diminish this effect the mind has. Given that the intellect is particularly unsuited to negotiate the present moment, which is our interface with the unknown, then we need to practice not knowing anything at all, not having beliefs or not holding strong opinions. All of these practices help us to step away from the domination of the mind and intellect and allow us to become masters of our own minds.

Exercise for Bringing the Mental Level into Balance

Exercise # 23: Acceptance

The purpose of this exercise is to help you practice staying present, aware and compassionate in all circumstances. If you find yourself becoming reactive, simply breathe and focus on your alignment for a few moments until you regain your balance and equanimity. Remember that to be in a place of acceptance is not the same thing as agreement. Acceptance is the acknowledgment of what is. Gregg Braden has written in <u>Walking Between The Worlds</u>, that what the world needs now, is to be viewed with eyes of compassion. Remembering that the observer affects what is being observed, helps us know that this act alone is of great value. When we can stay very present, holding a high frequency of consciousness in the face of the fear, confusion and separation that are screaming across the planet, we are true emissaries of peace. This exercise is healing for both you and the world.

Close your eyes and take three cleansing breaths. Inhale through your nose and draw your breath deeply into your belly. Slowly breathe out through the mouth. Do this three times. Open your alignment, grounding to the Earth and connecting with your crown chakra. Now breathe into your heart and rest there, in stillness and peace.

Imagine in whatever way you are able— seeing, sensing, feeling— that before you is an early spring morning, just at dawn. Feel the light and quiet that is there at this time of day. Say to yourself, "Yes, I am present. I see." Now let the image change and see a young child, pedaling her tricycle down the sidewalk, intent and happy. "Yes, I am present. I see." Now image the clear, crisp light of a fine autumn day. The clarity of the sky. The beauty of the colorful leaves. The brilliance of the sun. The scent of fall in the air. "Yes, I am present. I see." The image changes again and you are in a winter fairyland, just after a snow. The trees shimmer with crystals of frozen water that coat each limb. There are diamonds of ice shining everywhere and the world is magical. "Yes, I am present. I see." Now there is a steaming cup of tea, warm and cozy. "Yes, I am present. I see." Now you are in rush hour traffic. Cars are honking. "Yes, I am present. I see." The image changes and you see a young fawn, standing on wobbly legs, peering from the edge of a meadow. "Yes, I am present. I see." Now you see a happy baby, laughing. Eyes shining. "Yes, I am present. I see." Now the image changes and the baby is a starving infant, eyes dull and despairing. "Yes, I am present. I see." Breathe. Stay in your heart. Yes, there are these things in the world and I will look at them and know they are there. The image changes once again and you see two young people, holding hands and looking into each others eyes, joyful and adoring. "Yes, I am present. I see." Now you see a red cardinal on a branch, singing for its mate. Hopping and singing. "Yes, I am present. I see." The image changes and you see the Twin Towers, just as the second plane hits. "Yes, I am present. I see. I let my presence, my love and compassion touch everything, everything I see." Go slowly. Breathe. Return to the first image of the dawning spring day. Breathe. Now dissolve all the images. Breathe. Focus on your alignment and the light that moves through you. Breathe more light. Become a window for compassion, for the truth of light and let this shine out, illuminating the world. Slowly open your eyes and hold your presence as you do.

Mind As Servant

The mind has been described as a horse with the bit in his mouth that has no interest in listening to what the rider wants. Once the rider has gotten the bit where it belongs, then the rider directs the horse and not the other way around. Once we are in charge of our mind, it becomes the servant it was supposed to be. This powerful worker gives us our capacity to focus without attachment and hold as witness consciousness. When we go beyond mind as the ultimate reference point, worlds open for us in terms of who we know ourselves to be and what we are capable of creating.

Part of the manifestation process is the ability to hold a focus in both an immediate and long term sense. For example, if I am holding an inner ideal of peace, I can evaluate or measure actions, choices and beliefs against this ideal. If I remember to use beginner's mind, so that my ideal stays real and fresh, it does not become my story or idea about peace. Then the learning becomes an open-ended process where not only do I bring more and more of my life into alignment with this consciousness, but my understanding of this state of being continues to expand and deepen. Focus, thus, is important both for the big picture and the details.

Focus is also intimately involved with motivation and how I focus my mind can often determine what I will and will not do. Many years ago my family moved to a new home and I soon discovered that the room where I slept was quite cold. For the first time I found myself having trouble getting out of bed in the morning. All the stress which comes with not having enough time to get ready for the day was upon me. This situation persisted for a week or so and one morning I began to watch my mind as I lay snuggled in my warm bed. There was a parade of images of me shivering in the bathroom, my feet touching a cold floor, goose bumps on my arms, my body tight and tense against the unwelcome coldness in the room. The more I looked at these images, the better the bed felt. When I could delay getting up no longer, I had one last image of hurtling myself out of everything warm and good and into a cold, unpleasant world. The next morning as an experiment, I changed the focus. Now I deliberately saw a steamy bathroom and myself in a hot shower. A mug of good warm tea floated in front of me. I saw myself dressed and bustling about, happy with the day in front of me. There was no difficulty getting out of bed. I bounded up and was shocked at the difference a little change in focus made to my experience. This story is a long way of saying that if you are having problems motivating yourself, a good place to begin is by taking a look at the images and pictures that are going on in your mind. Consciously choosing what you are focused on can dramatically change what you are willing to do. Your mind is going to be focused on something. The power you have is in determining the focus. The more emotionally provocative the images are, the more compelling they will be because as noted earlier, feelings fuel us. This effect can be negative or positive. We can have strong fear images that paralyze us if we are reactive or we can have strong positive images that beckon us on in our creative endeavors. The mind is a great projectionist and often so skillful, we can get lost in what it projects. However, if we are able to put the intellect and mind back into its true role, then we will be in the position of telling the projectionist what movies to run and when to run them. We will also be free to not have stories at all and when we spend enough time free of pictures and stories, we begin to apprehend true reality.

Spiritual Confusion

Distortions and Filters

There are several areas of what may be termed spiritual confusion. Beyond the fact that we live in a culture that in large part has not bridged the chasm between spirituality and science and that many people are ambivalent about the idea that spiritual dimensions even exist, many of those who do believe in God carry a deep-seated fear of Spirit. I have found that often this apprehension is not conscious but it affects the energy field and the relationship with Spirit nonetheless. These fears can have several sources. First, there may be childhood images of God that are frightening. In western tradition the old testament image of God is quite terrifying. To paraphrase what Alan Watts once so irreverently said, "If your neighbor behaved as badly and as rudely as that God, you wouldn't have him over for supper." We can have many images of God. Our adult mind may say, "God is good and benevolent," and our subconscious can hold an image of a wrathful old man ready to send down punishment and retribution. A number of people have told me that they believe in a loving and merciful God, but when I look at their energy fields, their crown is closed up nice and tight. There is little chance that much is going to get through to them from the upper realms and the reason is because of the presence of fear.

Sometimes we unconsciously attribute to God characteristics that we experienced in our parents when we were children. So if our parents were untrustworthy, flawed or unforgiving, then we will tend to assume God is too. Psychologically our parents were once gods to us. Unfinished business is not only projected onto the people around us but it is also placed at the feet of God. This effect is so powerful that any serious spiritual work absolutely requires that we resolve these childhood issues and move passed them.

The fact that God is viewed in western culture as male can also have ramifications for women on their spiritual journey. When a woman attempts to find divinity within herself, she must deal with cultural messages that attribute the downfall of humans to a woman who ate an apple and depict the image of the sacred only in male form. As spiritual traditions of the east and west have begun to meet, women have the opportunity to be touched by the power of the divine feminine form. Quan Yin, the Chinese goddess of compassion, and the Hindu goddesses, Durga, Saraswati and Lakshmi are examples of feminine divinity. With the exception of Mother Mary we have not had much exposure to this spiritual aspect in our mainstream western culture. Cultural limitations on the understanding of the Divine and unfinished childhood issues both contribute to confusion about Spirit.

And lastly, in our very mental culture, it should not be a surprise that much more emphasis is placed on understanding God intellectually and conceptually than on actually experiencing the Divine directly. God can never be reached through the intellect because Spirit is beyond mind. Talking and conceptualizing about God is not the spiritual journey.

Fear of Change

We can also be afraid of God because we fear what Spirit will ask of us. When I speak with people about this issue, they often immediately assume that first, they will lose all their earthly possessions and then their close relationships. Spirit might also inflict some terrifying physical illness. Most of us remember the story of Job.

These images always involve change and it is interesting that the assumption is usually that the change is going to be painful. Certainly the mind is very fearful of change because change takes us into the unknown. Spirit does bring change and Spirit does take us into the realm of the unknown. Growth is a constant process of leaving old patterns of understanding and ways of being and embracing new ones. This is the path until we finally arrive at the essence of all that is—God. What must be stripped away are our attachments and not necessarily the possessions and relationships themselves. Sometimes the walk is through the fire as the Sufis say, and sometimes it is through the garden.

In this life not everyone is called to take this journey to God. But if you are, then the short route is to let the heart lead the head, for you will be inevitably invited into the mystery of the unknown over and over again. If this is your path, then why would Spirit not support you in every way? As humans we understand that if we want someone to succeed, we must not thwart the effort. Why do we think Spirit is less intelligent than that?

Mistrust as an Isolator

Trust can be a profound spiritual issue for if we do not trust Spirit, we are alone. If we do not trust or respect Earth and nature, then we are not supported in our journey. Separation and isolation are the most painful of human conditions. Mistrust is insidious and can cut us off from our own hearts, from our bodies, from earth and heaven and from life itself. Some of us have difficulty with our connection to heaven and some of us have problems with our connection to Earth. There are those that have a fear of both worlds and for them there is no place to go. Energetically fear causes contraction at all levels and cuts us off from that which is life engendering.

Fear roots itself in the soil of mistrust and can grow strange and twisted fruit. Love starts to appear as the enemy and peace a dangerous sophomoric state. Anxiety becomes a source of protection in an unpredictable world. This distortion of course is insanity itself. We must be aware of when we are participating in this insanity. Understanding the nature of our physical body, our heart, our mind and soul helps us to know how to work with our self. We have the tools to increase our clarity through aligning our Core. We have the power of the witness and the transformative flame of the heart. We carry within our own system the trinity of the Mother-Father God, the Holy Presence and the Divine Child. Thus we move beyond the forest of illusions created by our own and others fear minds, extricating ourselves from everything that is not truth. There is a path back to our essential essence and what will illuminate that path is the light of our own soul. The soul has chosen to bring Spirit into form. Believe in that choice.

Spiritual Maturity

There is a call from Spirit now to step into spiritual maturity. Following rules and being good is not enough. We are being asked to become responsible for ourselves and what we create in the world. This responsibility entails bringing balance and clarity into our own energetic systems for the purpose of co-creating with the Divine. This task requires deep listening to our own souls for it is here that the visions and dreams of what may be are held. Spiritual maturity means that we understand who we are and who we are not, what our role is and what it is not. This understanding creates true humility.

We are being asked to be intimate with God. Intimacy requires that we do not look to the other as a child to a parent, nor do we seek to run a private agenda and impose our will. Partnership is a dance of respect, self-responsibility, love and truth. What is opened and held between the lover and the beloved becomes the guiding force, the wave the dancers ride. In this partnership, giving and receiving become one. To connect deeply with Spirit is to come home. To connect with Spirit in human embodiment is to come home now and to afford the Divine a new form of expression. To live life from the place of the sacred is to be fully alive.

This notion of partnership is a new frontier and it is our charge to discover what it truly means. We are moving through a spiral of unending wholeness. The solar-lunar dance of unity holds both the divine hierarchy and the sacred webbed connection of all that is. Herein lies the mystery and paradox of who we are.

Exercise # 24: Infusing with the Christos

This exercise is particularly good to do because you are accessing the frequency point found in the tenth chakra that allows the mind to disconnect from the past. This switch stops referencing from patterns of the past and allows you to reference from your potential, which is not in the future but in the present moment. You will need to activate your vertical alignment to do this exercise effectively. When you become proficient with this exercise, you will be able to do this very quickly. Using it before engaging in new behaviors or while making decisions can be very helpful. Overtime, you will activate this frequency permanently in your system and you will not have to keep reaching up for it, because the Christos will simply be there. You become the Christos.

Close your eyes and take three cleansing breaths. Center yourself and activate your vertical alignment, starting with your grounding. Open your crown, only as wide as your root and let your first and seventh chakras strongly connect. Breathe light into the tube or line that forms between the root and the crown. Let this tube or line widen and extend at deeply into the earth as it can. Now let your crown reach up to your eighth center and feel the entire alignment. Going in order, let your eighth reach up into the ninth chakra. Feel the entire alignment. Now reach with your ninth center into the tenth chakra. Go as high as you need to go. You will recognize the tenth center by its vibrational quality of compassion, love and mercy. If you are visual, you will see its quality of golden white light. This is the Christos, the pattern of Spirit in form which is the perfect human. Let this light cascade down through and around your physical body and fill your energetic body. Breathe and feel the presence of this frequency, this consciousness. You can also rest in your alignment and ask the Christos to restructure your system. Make the request and allow the reordering to occur. Breathe. Allow. Now drop to your cellular level and ask this frequency to anchor itself here. Breathe. Allow. Let this integrate. When you are ready, open your eyes.

May you know the wonderment of mystery, the depth of Divine love and the stillness of peace.

May you remember the light of your true being, as you dance the oneness that is weaving us all.

Appendix 1

Meditation

There are many forms of meditation but they all share a similar goal: to still the egoic mind in order to reach higher states of consciousness. Some types of meditation use a single focus in order to achieve stillness. The focus may be as simple as watching the breath or may involve repeating a phrase or mantra. The mechanics are basically the same. Bringing the mind back to the one point over and over again eventually allows the chatter to quiet down. Zen meditation uses an opposite tact. In this style the meditator accepts all sensory input equally, paying no more attention to one thing than the other. This practice is actually more difficult than the one-pointed focus method. Taking a class or finding a meditation teacher can be quite helpful.

If you haven't already begun to meditate, then now would be a good time to start. The practice of meditation is an important part of the spiritual journey. Over time it cleanses and releases stress. It also affords the practitioner mastery over the mind. No matter what method you choose, there are several points to remember in order to keep your meditation the most beneficial. First, you should only close your eyes for meditation if you have had a bowel movement. Meditation tends to draw energy upward and if you have not moved your bowels, you may bring toxins up into your upper centers. Second, try short sessions at first. Initially even five minutes may be a lot. Meditation should not become an ordeal. It is a gift you are giving yourself and an opportunity to connect with your divinity. Any sense of drudgery will not improve the effect of the experience. Every meditator comes up against resistance. Simply be gentle, honest and observe the resistance. You don't need to be co-opted by your resistance nor do you need to be directed by it. In the end there is only one good reason to meditate: because you want to. Find the place that wants to sit with your divinity. Then you will bring a purity to your practice.

If meditation gives you headaches, then stop practicing until you have a chance to do some detoxification with either cleansing diets or fasting. Any fasting for longer than three days should be supervised by a knowledgeable practitioner. Many meditators cleanse at least several times a year and report not only improved general health but much better meditative experiences.

Appendix 2

Cold Water Therapy

Have the bathroom comfortably warm. Space heaters make this practice much easier in the winter months. Sit in an empty tub and begin to fill the bath with tepid water. Rub your legs and abdomen vigorously. Once you are used to the tepid temperature, add more cold water. Continue rubbing your legs, lower back and abdomen. The water should not rise above your waist. Keep moving and rubbing. Make the water as cold as you can.

If you notice yourself contracting against the cold, relax. Meet the coolness. The release of body heat can actually be very pleasant if you don't fight the sensation. Some people like to make deep, forceful "H" sounds—HA—-HO—-HEE—-HEY. Start with 2-3 minutes and work up to 5-6 minutes. Daily cold water baths are best.

This practice can still the mind very quickly, allowing it to become calm and alert. I have had reports of this practice aiding sleep, reducing PMS symptoms, reducing hallucinations, improving complexion and lowering anxiety. Cold water therapy is an important tool for lowering apana and improving health.

Appendix 3

The Five Rites

There are several sources for instruction on how to do the Five Rites. You will find them in the books recommended on the Reading List or you may get them off the Internet. There are numerous sites for this information. At the time of publication of this manual, they were listed on the following web site: www.fivetibetanrites.com

I am recommending them for their effect on apana. You will see that there are many benefits attributed to these practices. Although I cannot vouch for them reversing the aging process as the literature claims, I have found that they make a significant difference in general energy level when practiced regularly.

Appendix 4

Tapping Therapy

Tapping Therapy or EFT (Emotional Field Therapy) is one of the new energy therapies. It works with clearing blockages and trauma from acupuncture meridians and I have found it to be quite effective for many people. Tapping Therapy has the extra benefits of being both safe and gentle. Brain scans have shown that it changes blood flow in the brain. When we become anxious, blood tends to pool in the center of the brain. This tendency explains why we can't think as clearly when we become frightened or anxious. There is simply less blood flow in the cerebral cortex which is where we do our thinking.

At the time of this publication, instructions for this simple and easy to learn technique were listed on the following web site: www.emofree.com

One suggestion I would make is to use this technique often. You don't have to wait until you are maxing out to make yourself more comfortable.

Appendix 5

The Use of Guided Imagery

When we image we make use of our internal senses. Just as we can externally hear, see, smell, taste, we can turn this sensory perception inward and become quite skilled at perceiving the internal realms. As our conscious connection to this level of ourselves strengthens we can become effective in not only perceiving but in giving direction to our inner world.

Imaging makes use of all the internal senses even though the word image conveys the idea of a visual experience. Using Imagery is one way to talk to and direct your subconscious mind and your subtle energy field. Imagery is the language of the subconscious. We encounter this way of speaking in our dreams and the spontaneous pictures or feeling senses that come to us in our waking state. So if we want to communicate to this part of ourselves we need to use the language of the listener.

Basic Guidelines for Imagery

1. When practicing imaging, too much will power can get in your way. Use your will lightly. Too much effort only creates tension. The idea is to use only enough will to hold the intention or directive clearly.
2. Allow the process to happen.
3. Avoid practicing when overly tired or after a meal.
4. Postpone analyzing or evaluating your experience until after you are finished with your imagery.
5. Practice holding the attitude of expectancy without expectation.
6. Concentrate on the feeling or sensation of the image as opposed to visual impression. By emphasizing the feeling you will tend to activate the heart center. Focusing on the visual aspect can engage the third center.
7. When you practice, keep your back as straight as possible so that you will have better energy flow along your spine.

Suggested Reading

Assagioli, Roberto, *Psychosynthesis*: A Collection of Basic Writings, Easlen/Viking Press, 1987.

Assagioli, Roberto, *The Act of Will*, Viking Press, 1983.

Braden, Gregg, *Walking Between the Worlds: The Science Of Compassion*, Radio Bookstore Press, 1997.

Childre, Doc, *Freeze Frame: One Minute Stress Management*, Planetary Publications, 1998.

Emoto, Masaro, *Messages from Water*, HADO Kyoikusha Co., Ltd. Japan.

Grey, Alex, *Sacred Mirrors: The Visionary Art of Alex Grey*, Inner Traditions International, 1990.

Govinda, Kalashatra, *A Handbook of Chakra Healing*, Konecky & Konecky, 2004.

Hanh, Thich Nhat, *Peace Is Every Step: The Path of Mindfulness in Everyday Life*, Bantam Books, 1991.

Hawkins, David R., *Power vs. Force: The Hidden Determinants of Human Behavior*, Veritas Publishing, 2004.

Kelder, Peter, *Eye of Revelation: The Original Five Rites of Rejuvenation*, Borderland Sciences Research Foundation, 1990.

Kornfield, Jack, *After the Ecstasy, the Laundry*, Bantam Books, 2000.

Johari, Harish, *Chakras: Energy Centers of Transformation*, Destiny Books, 1987.

Johnson, Robert A., *We: Understanding the Psychology of Romantic Love*, Harper San Francisco, 1983.

Johnson, Robert A., *Ecstasy: Understanding the Psychology of Joy*, Harper, San Francisco, 1989.

McTaggart, Lynne, *The Field: The Quest for the Secret Force of the Universe*, Harper Collins Publishers, 2002.

Magdalena, Flo Aeveia/ The Ones With No Names, *Sun Light on Water: A Manual for Soul-full Living*, All Worlds Publishing, 1996.

Mallasz, Gitta (transcriber), *Talking with Angels-Budaliget 1943*, Daimon Verlag, 1988.

Myss, Caroline, *Anatomy of the Spirit: The Seven Stages of Power and Healing*, Three Rivers Press, 1996.

Raheem, Aminah, *Soul Return: Integrating Body, Psyche and Spirit*, Aslan Publishing, 1991.

Salzberg, Sharon, *Loving-Kindness: The Revolutionary Art of Happiness*, Shambhala Publications, Inc. 1995.

Stone, Hal and Stone, Sidra, *Embracing Our Selves: The Voice Dialogue Manual*, Nataraj Publishing, 1989.

Talbot, Michael, *The Holographic Universe*, Harper Collins Publishers, 1991.

Tarrant, John, *The Light Inside the Dark*, Harper-Perennial, 1998.

Tolle, Eckhart, *The Power of Now*, New World Library, 1999.

Tolle, Eckhart, *Living the Liberated Life and Dealing with the Pain Body*, (audio series), Namaste Publishing, Inc. 2001.

Resources

To order additional copies of this book, purchase CDs or inquire about workshops, you may e-mail Karen Custer at:

TheEnergeticCore@aol.com

Contact information for Anthony Ayiomamitis:

Address: Anthony Ayiomamitis
Agapis 2
NEA PALATIA-OROPOU 19015
Greece

E-mail: anthony@perseus.gr

Web site: www.perseus.gr/Astro-Solar-Analemma-140000.htm

Contact information for Flo Aeveia Magdalena:

Address: All Worlds Publishing
P.O.Box 1462
New Britain, Ct 06050-1462

E-mail: Soulsys@sover.net

About the Artist

Wendy Chapin provided the art work for the illustrations. She is a classically trained artist who has focused on color theory and design. Ms. Chapin has been studying painting at the National Gallery of Art for the past twenty years. As an artist, she believes the original intention of art was to touch the divine and to bring Spirit into our physical world. She enjoys the alchemical process of working with pigment as it transforms into images of beauty and healing.

Water Crystals: Masuru Emoto I. H. M. General Institute Authorization Number ihm0502070073

About the Author

Karen Custer currently writes and teaches classes on Core Energetics and topics of consciousness in addition to maintaining a private practice in Energy therapy. She has worked with and trained professionals in alternative therapy techniques for almost two decades. Ms. Custer has studied a number of traditions from both the East and West and is known for her ability to synthesize and integrate different healing systems. She received her Masters degree in Social Work from the University of Maryland School of Social Work in 1983. Through her counseling practice, classes, workshops and retreats, her work has touched thousands of people.

Printed in the United States
76375LV00005B/1-150

9 781420 841978

Would you like to be able to keep a clear head and an open heart, not only in ordinary moments but in stressful situations as well?

Would you like simple, effective tools to help you maintain better levels of energy and stamina?

Is being able to have a greater sense of presence for both yourself and others one of your spiritual goals?

Would you like to know how to stay connected to your deep essence no matter what is happening around you?

If you are a highly sensitive person, would you like to know how to venture into crowded places without becoming tired or drained?

Care and Feeding of the Energetic Core is an exciting and in-depth book that explores the basics of your subtle energy system and teaches you remarkably effective techniques to support, balance and strengthen this vital part of you. Written by a healthcare practitioner who has worked with individuals and groups for more than two decades, Karen Custer brings a wealth of knowledge and practical information to her reader.

authorHOUSE™

ISBN 1-4208-4197-1

90000

9 781420 841978